THE GREEK HOUSE

© THE ARCHAEOLOGICAL SOCIETY AT ATHENS

22 Panepistimiou St., Athens 106072

Fax (01) 3644996

ISSN 1105-7785

ISBN 960-7036-73-5

Editor: Eleftheria Kondylaki-Kontou

Translation: Alexandra Doumas

FIRST PUBLICATION: ELENA WALTER-KARYDI, *Die Nobilitierung
des Wohnhauses. Lebensform und Architektur im spätklassischen
Griechenland (Xenia* vol. 35, 1994, Publ. W. Schuller). UVK
Universitätsverlag Konstanz.

Cover illustration:
Pella, 'House of Dionysos', north peristyle, view from the south.
Cover illustration:
Delos, warrior's mask and Medusa mask,
from the mural decoration (stucco reliefs).
Delos Museum.

THE ARCHAEOLOGICAL SOCIETY AT ATHENS LIBRARY No 171

ELENA WALTER - KARYDI

PROFESSOR AT THE UNIVERSITY OF SAARBRÜCKEN

THE GREEK HOUSE

The rise of noble houses
in Late Classical times

ATHENS 1998

Contents

Introduction

In the middle years of the fourth century BC, as the kingdom of Macedonia was increasing in might, the orator Demosthenes struggled to stir his fellow Athenians to action against the expansionist policy of Philip II. He reminded them repeatedly of their former glory, adding in commendation of their illustrious forbears: 'Such was their rank in the world of Hellas: what manner of men they were at home, in public or in private life, look round you and see. Out of the wealth of the state they set up for our delight so many fair buildings and things of beauty, temples and offerings to the gods, that we who come after must despair of ever surpassing them; yet in private they were so modest, so careful to obey the spirit of the constitution, that the houses of their famous men, of Miltiades or of Aristeides, as any of you can see that knows them, are not a whit more splendid than those of their neighbours. For selfish greed had no place in their statesmanship, but each thought it his duty to further the common weal' (V *Olynth*. 25 ff.; transl. J. H. Vince. Loeb library).

Demosthenes' words are no mere rhetoric: excavations have shown that there were indeed differences between the houses of the fifth and those of the fourth century BC. In the fifth-century *polis* (as in the Archaic) there were no houses that revealed the wealth, power, learning or good taste of the owner. This does not mean that rich and poor did not exist ... simply that the rich did not set themselves off by a particular type of house. They did so in other ways, such as the so-called *liturgies* – the discharge of public duties: equipping a ship and maintaining its crew, or sponsoring the chorus in a theatrical perfor-

Fig. 1. Athens. Two houses west of the Areopagus. 5th cent. BC.

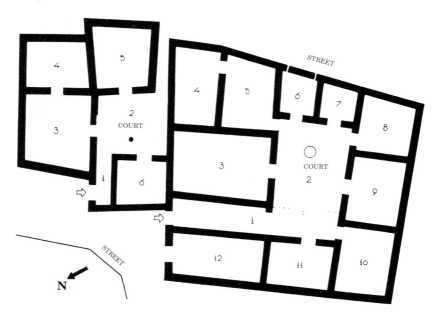

mance[1]. And if the performance were awarded first prize the sponsor (*choregos*) could commemorate this victory by setting up an *ex-voto* (costly, of course) to Dionysos, in a public place. In other words, this indirect taxation of the wealthy was motivated by the competitive spirit and the basic values of early Greek society: *honour* and *fame*. Cimon, for example, was popular in Athens because he executed his *liturgies* in a munificent manner: he allowed the poor free access to his estate and distributed rich charities (Aristotle, *Ath. Con.* 27, 3; Plutarch, *Cimon* 10, 1).

Fig. 2. Olynthos. Reconstruction of a house courtyard. View from the south.

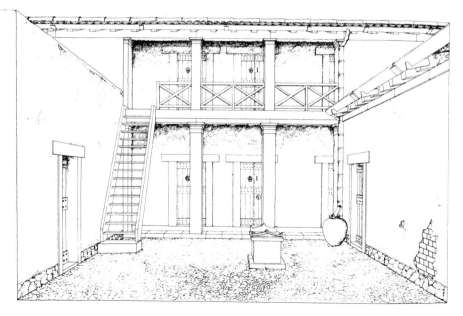

The rich also erected costly funerary monuments. These lined the roads leading out of the city, where there was considerable traffic, a constant reminder to passers-by of those buried there so they would not be forgotten. The worldly concern to be remembered and honoured after death was a prime one.

There were political offices that were not only unsalaried but also expensive for those assuming them. What was important was that they were honorary; they brought fame.

Such were the things on which wealthy Athenians, and Greeks in general, spent their money, until the end of the fifth century BC. Thus they established their identity as citizens, asserted themselves in the community and built up a good name.

This was obviously not the mentality that concerned itself with the beauty of the private house. Dwellings were built of cheap materials and were of simple plan, the rooms usually arranged around an inner courtyard (figs 1, 2).

In the closing years of the fifth century BC certain innovations were made in domestic architecture: the courtyard acquired a peristyle, the main rooms mural decorations and figural or ornamental floor mosaics[2]; moreover, for the first time marble sculptures were placed inside the house.

What prompted this change and how should it be understood?

Architecture

The principal innovation in architecture was the *peristyle court*. This was originally conceived for *public* buildings, such as the Pompeium, built outside the Dipylon gate of Athens around 400 BC (figs 3, 4)[3]. The rooms behind the colonnades of the court were used for banquets. Such halls, and even whole buildings (the so-called *hestiatoria*) for cult banquets, were a frequent feature of Greek sanctuaries. The Pompeium, though serving several functions, was primarily used for the Panathenaic Procession (*Pompe*), with which banquets were also associated. For this reason there were couches along the walls, as can be seen in the reconstruction drawing of a similar room in the South Stoa of the Agora (fig. 5).

Thus the peristyle court in private houses imitated that of public buildings such as the Pompeium. This is exemplified by an early fourth-century BC house at Eretria (fig. 6)[4]: a narrow corridor (c) leads from the entrance to the square peristyle court (a+b), around which are the rooms – the main ones on the north side, facing south and thus warm and light in winter and cool in summer, a detail to which the Greeks paid

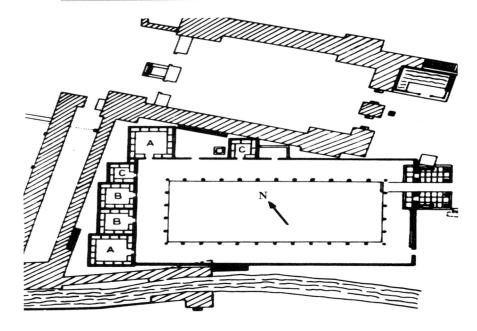

Fig. 3. Athens, Pompeium (A-C: banquet rooms). About 400 BC.

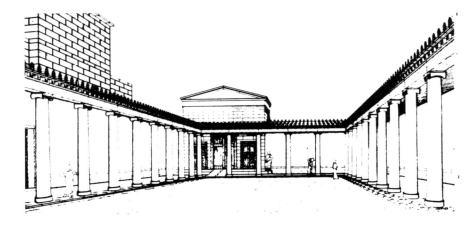

Fig. 4. Pompeium (fig. 3). The peristyle court.

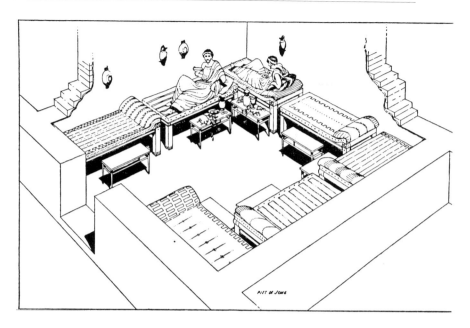

Fig. 5. Athens, Agora. South stoa I, banquet room. Late 5th cent. BC.

particular attention (Xenophon, *Memor.* III 8, 8.9; *Oeconomicus* IX, 4). The *andrones* (men's quarters) resembled the banqueting halls in public buildings (fig. 5). Here the master of the house entertained his friends; women were not admitted, hence these quarters were called *andrones*. In *andron* 9 (fig. 44) there were seven couches, *andron* 7 is larger, with 11 couches, and the smallest (5) has three (triclinium) (fig. 47). The high quality mosaics (figs. 45, 46), after which the house was named 'la maison aux mosaïques', as well as the polychrome mural decoration, only fragments of which have survived, distinguished the *andrones* from the other rooms. Apart from

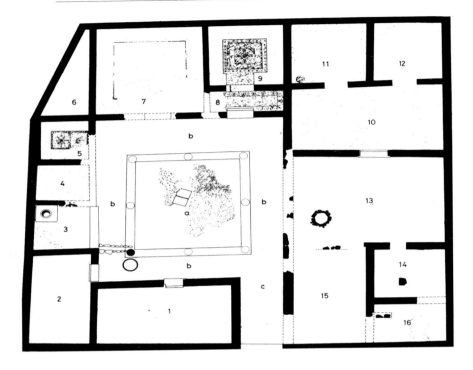

Fig. 6. Eretria, 'La maison aux mosaïques'. Early 4th cent. BC.

the *androdes*, the function of the other rooms in the house is often difficult to determine – and anyway must have been flexible[5]. The eastern part of the house was of secondary importance; there were no mosaics and the courtyard (13) had no columns; on the wall between the two parts of the house, now badly preserved, there will of course have been a doorway to the peristyle court.

Such a house indicates a profound change in the form of the domestic residence. Certainly houses without a peristyle court or with columns on just two sides, or even one side of the court, continued to be built. This is borne out by an insula in the city of Delos (fig. 7)[6]. The peristyle house (B) known as the 'House of Masks', from the subject of a high quality mosaic in the courtyard, is much larger than the other houses in the insula : the one with columns on only two sides of the courtyard (C) and the two houses with a simple courtyard without columns (A, D); moreover, there was at least one separate residence in the upper storey, as was usual in the densely populated city of Delos. Here the rich and the not so rich lived side by side.

Needless to say, no uniform type of house was established. In this more than in any other category of architecture, a certain licence prevailed : either hills or old streets that had to be taken into account imposed different plans, or earlier types of houses persisted, particularly in peripheral regions. In domestic architecture the old stood its ground against the new, and the marginal against the exemplary.

There were local differences too, not only in the building materials, which were what was most readily obtainable in each region, but also in the space available: the old cities were already densely built by the late sixth century BC, while in newly-founded cities there was plenty of space, permitting the application of a new architectural concept.

From the late fifth century BC onwards the courtyard *could* have columns, and a new architectural type was born, the so-called *peristyle house*. Peristyle houses were usually larger than the simpler dwellings, which were of course far more numerous, and distinguished also by mural decorations, floor mosaics and marble sculptures in their interior. So, henceforth, a *social*

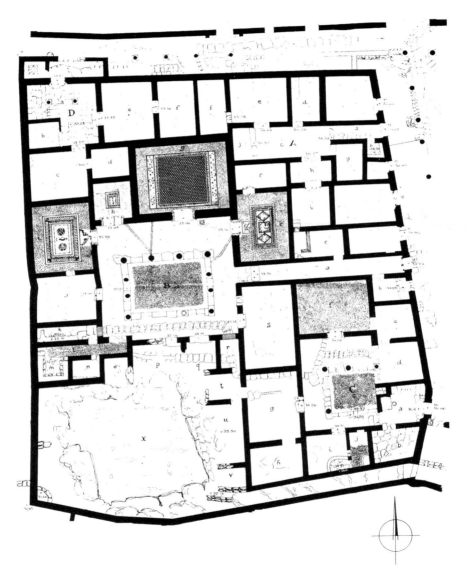

Fig. 7. Delos, insula of the 'House of the Masks'. Late 2nd cent. BC.

differentiation can be discerned in the morphology of the house. Whereas it had not been previously possible to recognize Miltiades' house, as Demosthenes pointed out (p. 1), it was now obvious which type of residence belonged to the high and mighty of the day.

With the peristyle the courtyard acquired an architectural form, becoming a space with an intrinsic value, constituting the heart of the house. The peristyle court could be square or oblong, but was always rectangular; the old, irregular court-yard forms disappeared. Peristyle or not, the court was always paved. An altar for domestic cult usually stood in it, but there were no trees or flowers. Pleasure gardens did not exist[7]. Such gardens, as it were a private staging of nature, were a creation of the Late Hellenistic period. The visual character of the peri-style court was essentially determined by the columns – and we know that in ancient Greece the column was an element of high architecture. Thus there was a morphological enhancement of the courtyard and of the private house as a whole, so that we can, for the first time, speak of 'noble houses'.

The peristyle court and the *androues* were the locus of the social life of the master of the house: drinking, feasting, discussing... The culmination of such gatherings were the scientific-philosophical colloquies, such as those admirably presented by Plato. Indeed, several Platonic dialogues took place in Athenian houses: the *Politeia* in Cephalos' house, the *Symposium* in Agathon's, the *Protagoras* in Callias'.

The *Protagoras* (314D ff.) begins with a description of how Socrates and a friend went to the house of the rich man Callias to seek out the Sophist Protagoras, who was a guest there along with Hippias and Prodicos. Plato presents a slightly sarcastic picture of the three Sophists: Protagoras strutting confidently back and forth in the front part of the peristyle court, surrounded by pupils and admirers; Hippias lolling comfortably in an armchair by the columns opposite, while his audience makes do with benches; they ask him questions 'about nature and celestial bodies', and he holds forth prolixly to each in turn by way of answer... Prodicos is still in bed, tucked in with blankets and furs, 'and plenty of them too' adds Plato derisively, in a room that was once a storeroom but has been turned into a guestroom, due to the host of guests. His listeners are likewise reclining on couches (here Plato parodies the *andron*!). Socrates draws Protagoras into conversation, Hippias and Prodicos come to join in; the listeners bring other benches and couches, and the dialogue can commence.

Apart from the irony with which Plato introduces the three Sophists, this text provides a picture of the unpretentious way of life in the peristyle court in those days. We learn from other literary sources that the family could spend its day here; male drinking parties, domestic cult, philosophical discussions all took place here. There was apparently no strict functional distinction of domestic areas, nor was there an etiquette.

The concept of the peristyle was further enhanced in houses with two such courts. This has been ascertained at Pella, capital of the Macedonian kingdom, which seems to have been the most splendid late fourth-century BC city in Greece.

Two houses, named after their mosaics[8] the 'House of Dionysos' (figs 8, no 1,10) and the 'House of the Rape of Helen' (figs 8, no 5,9,11), are of impressive size: whereas 'la maison

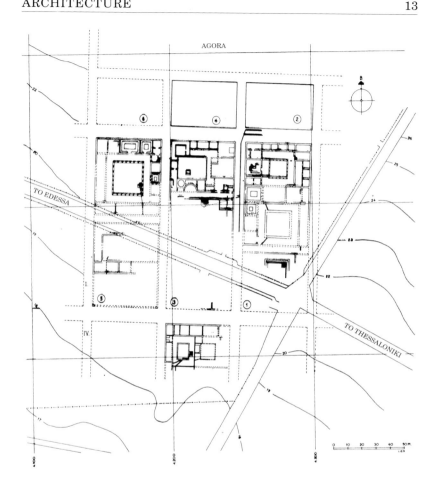

Fig. 8. Pella, area south of the agora.

aux mosaïques' at Eretria (fig. 6) is about 650 m² in area, the 'House of the Rape of Helen' is about 2350 m² and the 'House of Dionysos', which has two peristyle courts, reaches 3160 m².

The peristyle court in the 'House of the Rape of Helen' (figs 8, no 5,9,11) has limestone Doric columns at ground floor level

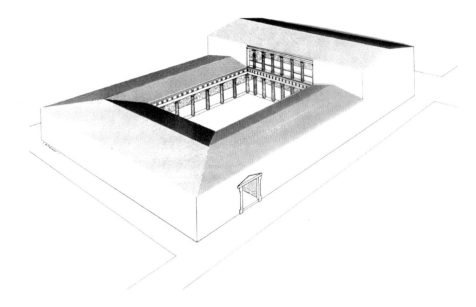

Fig. 9. Pella, 'House of the Rape of Helen' (fig. 8, no 5). About 330-320 BC.

and marble Ionic ones on the upper storey; of the rooms around it the western and southern ones are destroyed. In the northern part there are three *andrones*, in the middle one of which is the mosaic that gave its name to the house and in the eastern a masterly representation of a stag hunt signed by the artist (Gnosis made it); its counterpart, the mosaic in the western *andron*, is almost completely destroyed. The arrangement of *andrones* east of the peristyle court is different: there are two of them, accessible through a middle anteroom with a mosaic of the Amazonomachy (fig. 11)[9].

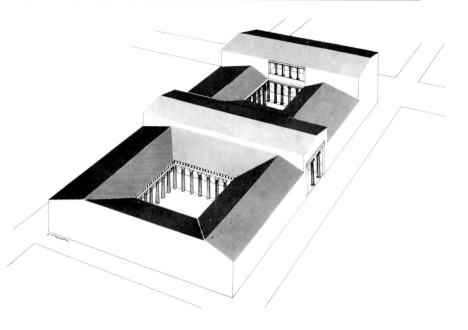

Fig. 10. Pella, 'House of Dionysos' (fig. 8, no 1). About 330-320 BC.

No windows have been restored in the two maquettes (figs 9,10) because there are no certain indications of their position. As a rule house windows were small, plain and set high up, as in the reconstruction of an *andron* at Priene (fig. 12), or in a house at Orrhaon (Ammotopos), where the walls are preserved to an appreciable height (fig. 13)[10]. It should also be stressed that such windows were a characteristic morphological feature of the ancient Greek house: openings used mainly to let in light and fresh air. The *view* as a value in its own right was discovered later, in the first century BC, determining the form of a

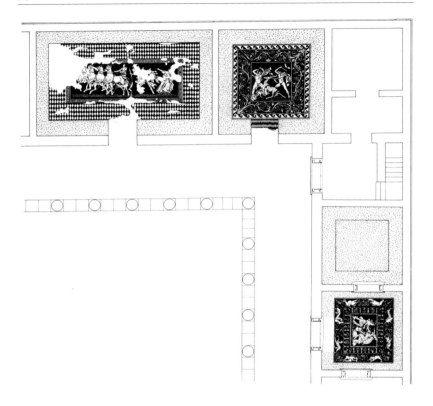

Fig. 11. Pella, 'House of the Rape of Helen' (figs 8, no 5,9). Northeast corner.

new, Late Hellenistic domestic architectural type: the villa[11].

Most of the openings in the house faced inwards, onto the courtyard: doors, windows, even double windows furnished with the ennobling element of a column (fig. 14). Sometimes, the whole front of an *andron* wall was replaced by columns on a podium (fig. 15), in order to admit more light and air.

The small *andron* at Priene (fig. 12) was a triclinium, like its

Fig. 12. Priene, reconstruction of an andron.

Eretrian counterpart (fig. 6, no 5,47). In the houses at Pella things were on another scale: the *andron* with the Rape of Helen mosaic (fig. 11) was furnished with 19 couches! Obviously no ordinary citizens resided here but the powerful dignitaries of the Macedonian state, perhaps the king's *hetairoi* (companions). The symposia held here were legendary; when Douris of Samos accused Demetrios Phalereus of loving a luxurious life

Fig. 13. Epirus, Orrhaon (Ammotopos). House I. Second half of 4th cent. BC.

while imposing austerity on the Athenians, he stressed that
Demetrios outshone even the Macedonians in the lavishness of
his banquets[12]!

In the 'House of Dionysos' (figs 8, no. 1; 10) both courtyards
are peristyle ones, whereas in 'la maison aux mosaïques' (fig. 6)
the second courtyard had no columns and was of secondary importance. Moreover, the position of the entrance between the
two peristyles (figs 8, no. 1; 10) – the north one Ionic (cover
illustr.), the south Doric – indicates that equal value was
attached to both. West of the south peristyle is a group of rooms
just like those in the 'House of the Rape of Helen' (figs 8, no.

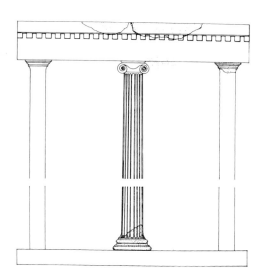

Fig. 14. Eretria, 'La maison aux mosaïques' (fig. 6). Reconstruction of a window.

5,11): two *androndes* with an anteroom between; the mosaic of Dionysos, after which the house was named, was in the north *andron* (fig. 51)[13] and the lion hunt mosaic (fig. 50) in the one behind the entrance[14].

So the peristyle concept is fully elaborated, indeed extolled in the spacious houses of Pella. Comparison with the courtyard in fig. 2 shows the morphological modification of these areas, their express pretensions. Indeed it could be that peristyle courts with two storeys not only on one but on all four sides already existed in Pella at this time. One such court has been found in an imposing house at Monte Iato (fig. 16)[15], of about

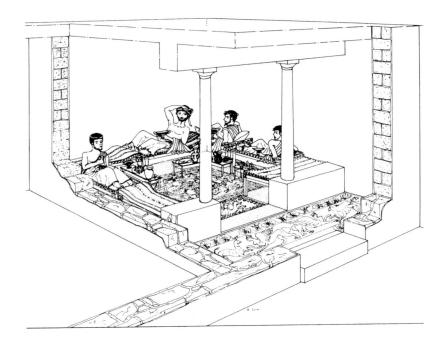

Fig. 15. Eretria, 'La maison aux mosaïques' (fig. 6). Andron 8 and 9.

300 BC, yet it is more likely that the second storey on the peristyle in domestic architecture was a Macedonian creation, thereafter adopted in Sicily, than a Sicilian one. The combination of a Doric colonnade on the ground floor with a lighter Ionic one on the upper floor (fig. 16) had already appeared in the 'House of the Rape of Helen' (fig. 9) and was henceforth to become the norm.

Two-storey peristyle courts, such as fig. 16, were not unusual in the Hellenistic period. In the densely built Late

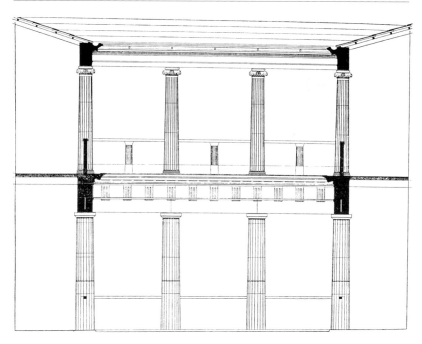

Fig. 16. Sicily, Monte Iato. House I, two-storey peristyle court. About 300 BC.

Hellenistic city of Delos there are two– and even three-storey peristyle courts that are sometimes so small they look more like lightwells (fig. 17a-b): whatever the restrictions of space, people wanted the peristyle, they insisted on having a noble house.

In Macedonia of Alexander the Great conditions were ideal for promoting the type of the peristyle house (figs 8-11): there were people affluent enough to afford such houses, there was the vigour of a young state and, last but not least, building land was still available. In the great old cities such as Athens the

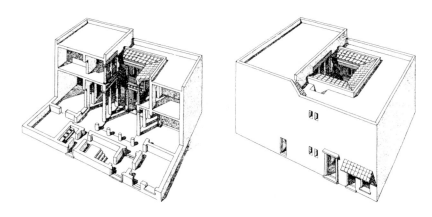

Fig. 17a-b. Delos. Reconstruction of a house (H. Schleif).

Fig. 18. Athens, 7 Menandros St. Andron and anteroom of a house. Early 4th cent. BC.

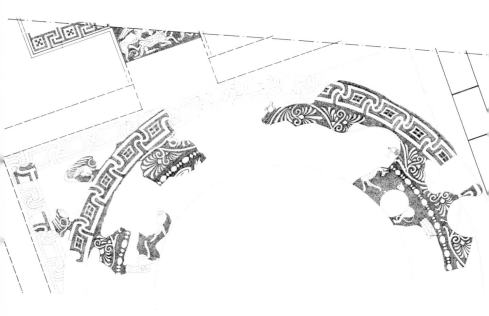

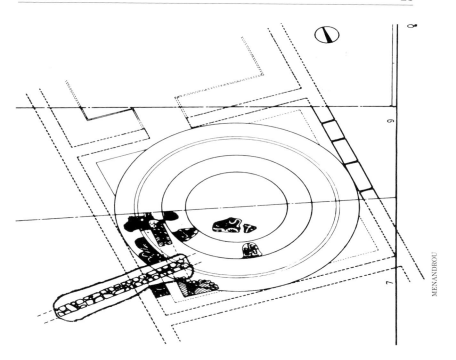

Fig. 19. Andron and anteroom (fig. 18) with parts found later (9 Menandros St.), reconstruction.

density of settlement was such that it was hardly possible to find plots suitable for such spacious residences.

Even though the excavation of domestic quarters is fraught with difficulties in present-day Athens, some examples have been investigated. A particularly significant find is an *andron* with anteroom (figs 18-19)[16], which certainly belonged to a stately peristyle house of the early fourth century BC. Only part of the *andron* is preserved, with the threshold mosaic, but the anteroom can be reconstructed on the basis of the mosaic, as a square one of side 9.20 m. This was clearly not an *andron* with a narrow room in front, as for example in 'la maison aux mosaïques' (figs 6, no. 8-9; see also fig. 44); although the entrance to the anteroom was not found the whole may have been a suite of three rooms (anteroom between two *androndes*) similar to those frequently found in Macedonia in the second half of the fourth century BC (see p. 19). Indeed it is striking that in the 'House of the Rape of Helen' the anteroom with the Amazonomachy mosaic (fig. 11) is smaller than the one in figs 17,18 and the corresponding room (F) in the palace at Vergina (fig. 21, E-F-G) is only slightly larger (approximately 10x10 m.). This gives some idea of the scale of the rooms in this Athenian house, which must have had a peristyle court.

This noble house stood on the northern edge of Athens, close to the city wall[17]. A second peristyle house was found nearby[18]. It seems then that on the outskirts of the city, near the wall, building land for spacious houses was still available, while in the centre settlement was dense; many artisans and tradesmen were installed in the vicinity of the Agora, their workshops and shops crowded along the narrow, winding streets[19]. This was not of course a hard and fast rule, since the aristocratic neighbourhood of Melite, where the wealthy Callias had his house (see p. 93f.), was not far from the Agora.

Lack of space must indeed have been a problem for those Athenians who wanted to live in noble style, and it is often ascertained in excavation that someone acquired his neighbour's house in order to gain space: perhaps the peristyle house (fig. 20) built in the late fourth century BC on top of two earlier houses without peristyle court, is one such case. Furthermore,

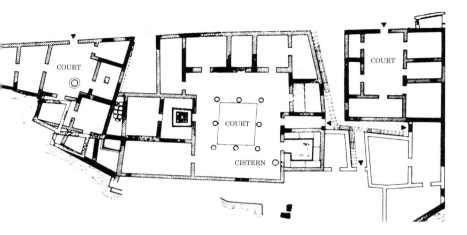

Fig. 20. Athens, northeast slope of the Areopagus. Houses of the late 4th cent. BC.

it seems that the comic poets of these years made fun of those who, among other things, added a peristyle court to their house, either to copy their neighbour or to show off to him[20].

To digress a little. In Macedonia the type of the peristyle house was also used for the *royal palace*. Two fourth-century BC palaces are known: at Vergina (Aegae)[21] and Pella. Since excavation of the colossal complex at Pella, which was the main palace of the Macedonian kings, is still in progress[22], we shall look at the building in Vergina (figs 21,22).

Its original form was that of a house with one peristyle court (the small western one was added later), but of enormous dimensions, over 9200 m^2 (that is larger by far than the 'House of Dionysos' at Pella). But it is not merely size that distinguishes the royal palace from the private peristyle houses; the morphological distinction is significant too: the palace has a

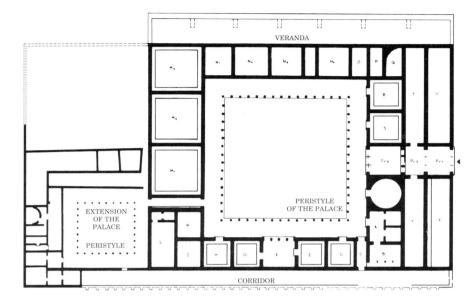

Fig. 21. Vergina, palace. About 330-320 BC.

colonnaded front as well as a monumental *entrance*. Thus the two architectural types – palace and peristyle house – are clearly distinguished; this must be stressed because sometimes stately peristyle houses are called 'palaces'.

Another comparison is significant. In the fifth century BC not only the private houses had a plain exterior, but also the *public edifices*. This is apparent, for example, in the reconstruction of the west side of the Agora (fig. 23). The temple of Hephaestus is peripteral and further enhanced by the pedimental sculptures and the acroteria, while the public buildings have plain exteriors, without columns and with small windows set high up.

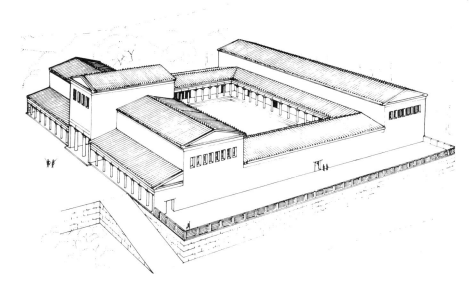

Fig. 22. Palace (fig. 21). Reconstruction (D. Pandermalis).

This morphological differentiation should not be understood
as one between sacred and profane architecture, because the
Greeks did not sharply distinguish between the sacred and the
secular. No building was without an altar, whether it was
intended for physical exercise (palaestra, gymnasium...) or for
civil administration (prytaneum, bouleuterium...), or even a
house, in which case the altar usually stood in the courtyard
(fig. 2). Whatever the activities in these buildings, religious
rites were always a part of them. Even the symposium – not
just the cult feast in the sanctuary but revels at home with
one's friends – began with a hymn and a libation to the gods.
Nothing took place without the gods.

Fig. 23. Athens, Agora. West side. Late 5th cent. BC (W. Dinsmoor Jr.).

The reason for the morphological difference between the temple and the aforementioned buildings is rather that in these it was the *inner space* – whatever its function – that was important. The temple, on the contrary, did not have an inner space with an intrinsic value. This is evident from cult practices, for rites were not performed *inside* the temple but *in front* of it, at the altar. The temple is an architectural *body*, the kernel of which is the cult statue in the cella; the pteron constitutes, as it were, its corporeal limit. On account of this bodily quality the temple is a characteristic Greek architectural creation, and was undoubtedly the pinnacle of architecture for the Greeks themselves.

The axiomatic scaling of buildings is indicated too in the

construction, the choice of materials and other features; it is not necessary here to enter into details.

However, it is significant that the creation of noble houses occurred at about the same time as the rise of noble public buildings of assembly. The peristyle court and the floor mosaic pictures appeared in the latter only slightly earlier than in the former. There is however a difference: the public buildings also acquired a noble *exterior*. From the fourth century BC onwards they frequently had colonnaded fronts, and in some instances columns were even added to an existing edifice. The *bouleuteria* at Olympia are a case in point; in the mid-fourth century BC an Ionic colonnade was added to these two late sixth-century BC council halls, unifying their front (fig. 24).

The enhancement of the exterior of public buildings in the fourth century BC culminates in the Leonidaeum (fig. 25). In Roman times the building was used as the quarters of the Roman *dioecetes* (governor) of Greece (Pausanias 5, 12, 2), and most probably its original function was analogous, as a guest-house for important pilgrims to the sanctuary, with rooms for symposia[23]. Its morphological enhancement is impressive: not only is the Leonidaeum the largest building in the great pan-hellenic sanctuary, it also combines the peristyle court, around which the rooms are arranged, with external colonnades on all four sides – in other words it is peripteral like the temples: something unimaginable before the fourth century BC!

It could be argued that, as a dedication, the Leonidaeum participates in the sanctity of the place, it is 'ἱερὸν Διὸς' (sacred to Zeus), as the *ex-votos* are characterized. This does not, however, explain its architectural form. The *Lesche of the Cnidians*

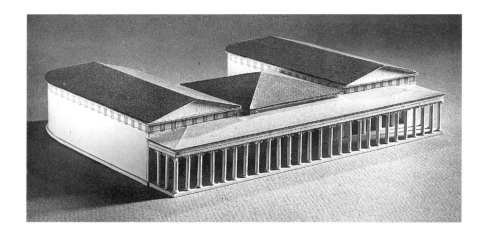

Fig. 24. Olympia, bouleuteria (maquette). Mid-4th cent. BC.

Fig. 25. Olympia, view of the sanctuary from the west (maquette); left in front the Leonidaeum.

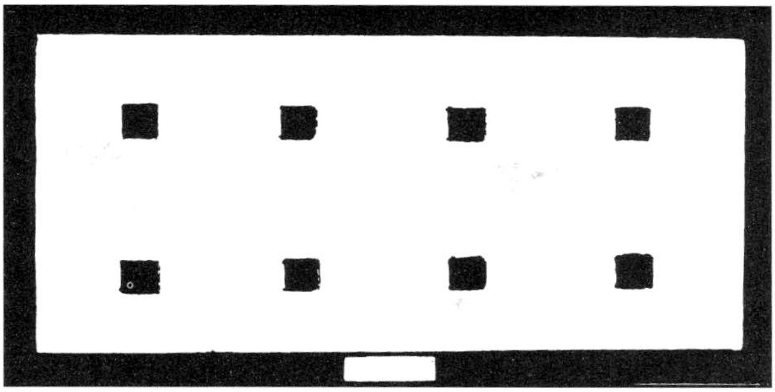

Fig. 26.
Delphi.
Lesche of the
Cnidians.
About 460-
450 BC.

(fig. 26) is also a dedication in a sanctuary, but its exterior is quite plain. The morphological difference between the two buildings can be explained by their dates: the *Lesche* was built shortly before the mid-fifth century BC, that is at a time when buildings of assembly had plain exteriors. In this respect the Lesche resembled the public buildings in the Athenian Agora (fig. 23).

It is a striking fact that prior to the Leonidaeum there was no building in the greatest panhellenic sanctuary for the accommodation of the rich and powerful. As a rule the pilgrims stayed in tents, and whoever wanted to cut a dash simply saw to it that his temporary abode was a splendid one, as did Alcibiades and Dionysios I of Syracuse. Even that shocked the Greeks. When Alcibiades came to Olympia to take part in the games, his tent was Persian and so sumptuous that it outshone all the Athenians there could boast together. This is one of the episodes that shows how Alcibiades roused and riled his fellow citizens, giving them good reason to believe that he sought to overthrow the democracy and make himself tyrant[24].

Thus the Leonidaeum (fig. 25) can be qualified as a 'noble guest-house'. Morphologically, however, it represents an extreme case, which was not continued. Hellenistic public buildings display various distinguishing features on their exterior, but they are never peripteral (cf. e.g. fig. 37).

We can conclude that the rise of noble houses concurred, as it were, with the rise of noble public buildings for assembly, the design of which became a prime concern of Hellenistic architects. Peristyle houses did indeed imitate, or rather emulate such public buildings, but they did not overstep certain limits. In contrast to public buildings their exterior remained plain throughout the Hellenistic era (fig. 16); they had neither columns or even half-columns, nor an elaborate entrance. In other words: even in the Hellenistic city an individual's house should not stand out from those of his fellow citizens. The ennobling of the house was confined to its interior.

Let us take a look at the interior of the peristyle houses.

Mural decorations

Both the connections and the differences between the architecture of peristyle houses and public buildings are expressed in the mural decorations, which too made their appearance around 400 BC.

The reconstruction of a Late Hellenistic wall (fig. 27)[25] gives us an idea of fourth-century BC ones as well, because this kind of decoration did not change substantially until the beginning of the first century BC, that is until the so-called Second Pompeian style. Panels of various colours render *isodomic masonry.*

Only fragments of early mural decorations of this kind have survived (note 25). Nevertheless, these clearly indicate that polychromy prevailed from the outset; monochrome walls (where the courses were rendered only by incision) were rare, or rather occurred in modest residences. Likewise from the outset, the masonry was represented not only with colour but also, as a rule, with applied stucco. The role played by this relief

Fig. 27. Athens. Mural decoration. Late 2nd-early 1st cent. BC.

rules out the term wall-painting; it is better to speak of *mural decoration*, in which colour and moulding are equal partners.

The theme of this decoration is the *ashlar masonry wall*. This may seem strange, yet has a quite reasonable explanation. The walls of private houses were constructed as a rule of sun-dried bricks or rubble masonry –cheap materials– on a stone socle. Ashlar blockwork was reserved for monumental architecture.

Let us consider as an example of a public building the northern part of the Propylaea, which J. Travlos identified as an *hestiatorion* (figs 28,29)[26], that is a hall for banquets with couches along its walls (cf. fig. 5). The structure of the marble wall (fig. 28) is the model imitated or represented with colour and stucco relief in domestic mural decorations. The components of the walls in figs 27 and 28 are the same: from the bottom upwards, a low socle, large panels – the so-called *orthostates–*, followed by the string course (*katalepter*) which, lying between the *orthostates* and the main zone of the wall, was emphasized, as is the norm for articulating elements in Greek architecture. Thus there occur here relief mouldings and painted ornaments or a figured frieze; in Late Hellenistic times there was frequently a multiplication of zones in the string course (figs 27,30,32,33,35), but figured friezes are found here already in early examples[27]. Above the string course is the main field: a series of regular courses of isodomic ashlar marble blocks in the hall of the Propylaea (fig. 28) and coloured stucco imitations of these on domestic walls (figs 30,32,33); at the top there are relief cornices, of marble (fig. 28) or of applied stucco (figs 27,32).

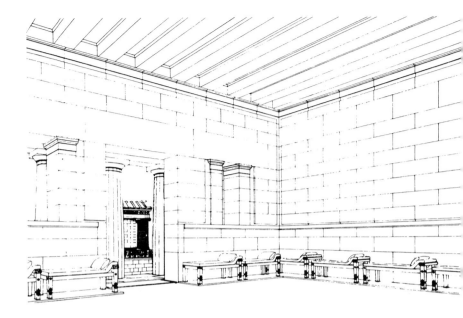

Fig. 28. Athens, Acropolis. Interior of the 'Pinakotheke' (J. Travlos). 437-432 BC.

In other words, this mural decoration did not just represent the structure of a wall but specifically the ashlar masonry of *monumental architecture*; thus it visually assimilated the domestic interior to public buildings, just as the peristyle assimilated the courtyard of the house to the courts of public buildings.

This was certainly a conscious intention of the house owners and was treated as such by their detractors, such as Demos-

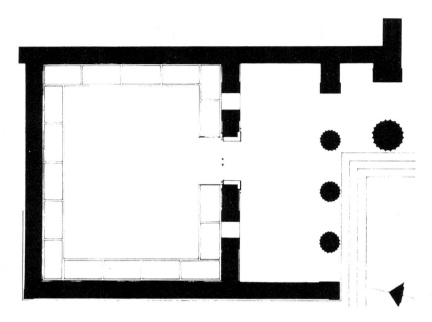

Fig. 29. Athens, Acropolis. Northwest side of the Propylaea (fig. 28).

thenes, who repeatedly censured such residences (p. 1), explicitly stating that 'In those old times [fifth century BC] the State was wealthy and splendid, but in private life no man held his head higher than the multitude ... Witness those gatehouses, docks, porticoes, the great harbour, and all the edifices with which you see the city adorned. But today every man who takes part in public life enjoys such superfluity of wealth that some of them have built private-dwelling houses more

Fig. 30. Delos, 'House of the Dolphins', room G. Mural decoration. Late 2nd cent. BC.

magnificent than many public buildings...' (*Against Aristocrates* XXIII 206-208; transl. J. H. Vince, Loeb library). And judging from the house in figs 18,19, Demosthenes was not far off the mark!

Nevertheless, as in architecture so too in mural decoration, differences existed between the domestic interior and public

Fig. 31. Vergina, chamber of the 'Tomb of Persephone', interior. North wall (A. Kottaridou). 340-330 BC.

buildings. There were limits in the house which nobody overstepped, the main one being that here no large pictorial wall-paintings appeared.

Monumental paintings were to be found, for example, in the stoas or public buildings of assembly; the renowned works by Polygnotos, *Iliou Persis* and *Nekyia*, in the *Lesche of the*

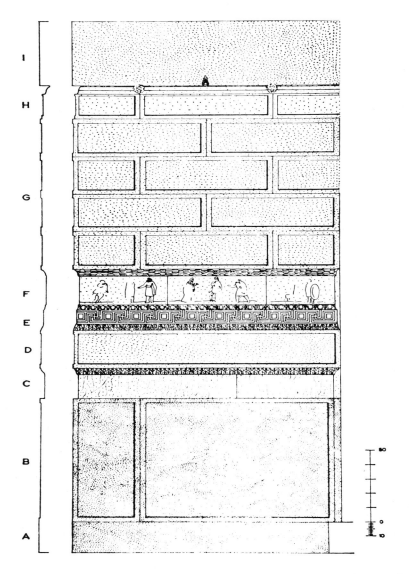

Fig. 32. Delos, 'House of the Actors', oecus N. Mural decoration. Late 2nd cent. BC.

Fig. 33. Athens. Mural decoration. Late 2nd-early 1st cent. BC.

Fig. 34. Vergina, chamber of the 'Tomb of Persephone' (fig. 31). The rape of Persephone.

Fig. 35. String course from the mural decoration of a house at Pergamon (reconstruction). 2nd cent. BC.

Cnidians are a case in point (fig. 26; Pausanias 10, 25-31). In the hall of the Propylaea too (figs 28,29), the main zone of wall above the string course was covered with pictures[28]. The painters of the fifth and fourth centuries BC, known to us from the literary sources, established their reputation through such works. On the contrary, domestic mural decoration was anonymous and cannot even be called a wall-painting, since colour and moulding played an equal role (p. 33ff.).

The story that Alcibiades wanted to adorn his house with paintings, and that he held the painter Agatharchos there by force, releasing him only when he had fulfilled his whim[29], fits in with all that is known about this outrageous personality who provocatively overstepped the mark that held for every Athenian citizen. This and similar incidents fuelled the charges that Alcibiades had ambitions of becoming tyrant (p. 31).

None of the famous ancient Greek paintings has survived; they are only known of from the texts. Yet some idea of what has been lost is furnished by the wall-paintings of the Macedonian tombs. There is nothing strange about the existence of works of high art in tombs, since for the ancient Greeks funerary monuments rose above the domestic domain. In the royal tombs at Vergina in particular, great monumental paintings are preserved. The 'tomb of Persephone' is an example, on three walls of the burial chamber of which the rape of the goddess by Pluto is represented (figs 31,34)[30].

The arrangement of the decoration under the main representation is the same as that on domestic walls: socle, *orthostates* and string course with blue-ground frieze of griffins which corresponds to the narrow (about 15 cm. high) figured friezes sometimes found in this position on house walls too (figs 30,32,35). In the upper part however, above the string course, the main theme, the large wall-painting of Persephone, occupies the position given over to isodomic masonry on domestic walls[31]. Moreover, it is significant that unlike the large, white-ground representations (e.g. fig. 34), the friezes of the string course are red -or dark (blue or black)- ground ones, these colours being used for the ground of secondary zones in mural decoration. In other words, these friezes did not play an important role in the decorative ensemble, either through size or colour (figs 30,32).

Even in domestic mural decorations of the highest quality there was no monumental painting. Thus for instance the string course of a wall from an outstanding peristyle house at Pergamon has, as is often the case in the second century BC, a multiplication of the decorative zones (fig. 35):[32] successive mouldings and ornamental bands, a griffin frieze (similar to that in the 'tomb of Persephone', fig. 34), as well as panels imitating ashlar blocks of different kinds of stone. And yet there was no wall-painting above this elaborate string course, just the typical representation of masonry: the whole followed the norm for domestic mural decoration.

Decoration such as this –the laborious application of stucco and the painting in various colours– so carefully executed and of such excellent quality, was by no means cheap. The absence of monumental pictures was not a measure of economy but a matter of principle: monumental painting had no place in the decoration of the house, just as external colonnades or a propylon had no place in its architecture. Such morphological

Fig. 36. Samothrace, sanctuary of the Cabeiri. Interior of the Hieron. Late 4th cent. BC.

features made evident that the citizen as an individual did not overstep certain limits in his house.

Mural decoration could only be enriched with more *architectural elements*, which too were references to public buildings. So, for example, there were lion heads (like the water spouts on the roof) and antefixes (fig. 32), or even relief triglyphs and metopes (fig. 33), sometimes indeed with relief or painted scenes[33]. Such references explicitly stressed the under-lying principle of the decoration as a whole, that its function was to assimilate visually domestic space to public space.

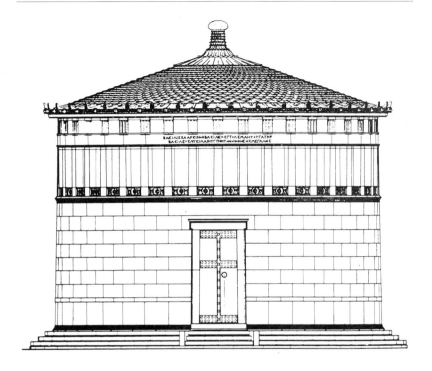

Fig. 37. Samothrace, sanctuary of the Cabeiri. Arsinoeum. Early 3rd cent. BC.

Another such reference were upper-wall relief mini-colonnades; a late second-century BC room decorated in this manner has been preserved intact at Pompeii[34], and here the colourful and sculptural, as well as the purely architectural character of such walls can be appreciated.

Polychromy as such was also something new in the private house, for it was until the end of the fifth century BC an ex-

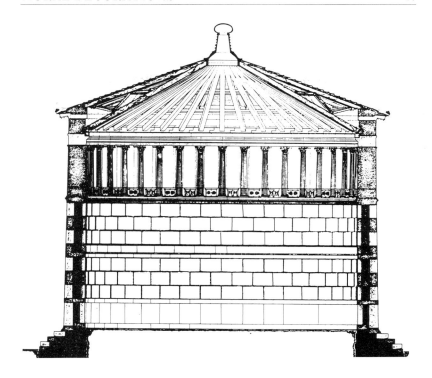

Fig. 38. Arsinoeum (fig. 37). Interior.

clusive feature of high architecture. However, polychromy in domestic space was used more lavishly: not only to pick out the relief elements of the wall decoration, emphasizing the structure, but also to create a festive ambience – in this respect deviating from the imitation of the exterior of public buildings.

There were mini-colonnades also on the walls of the Hieron on Samothrace (fig. 36), a building with temple-like exterior where the initiates of the cult of the Cabeiri gathered. Such assembly halls, and the *hestiatoria* too, frequently had the same mural decoration as the domestic *andrones* (which is why it is impossible to determine from the decoration alone whether the walls in figs 27,33 come from a renovation of the Pompeium or from nearby houses; note 25). The absence of large wall-paintings from the hall fig. 36 makes it look very like a domestic *andron*; thus we may assume that already in these years – and not for the first time in the second century BC, from which many examples have survived– domestic rooms had mini-colonnades such as the one in the hall fig. 36[35].

An analogous feature to the colonnades of fig. 36, or rather a development of the same decorative idea, is the false gallery of the Arsinoeum, a colossal assembly hall, a dedication of the Ptolemaic queen Arsinoe (figs 37,38): plain Doric piers on the outside, Corinthian half-columns on the inside, with reliefs between (parapets - altars), and thin marble plaques in the upper part. This is a characteristic Hellenistic decoration which ennobled both the exterior and the interior of the building (cf. on the contrary fig. 26). In the house, as we have seen, only the interior was ennobled; thus in a late third-century BC house at Pella the walls of an exedra have the decorative schema of the Arsinoeum: in the upper part white relief piers with red parapets, above these dark blue panels (fig. 39)[36]. The colours here are so well preserved that its original bright polychromy is virtually unsullied. The three, five-metre high walls with the same colourful architectural decoration, gave the exedra a festive air, as well as the character of a public space. 'Galleries' such as this are unequivocal expressions of the basic principle

Fig. 39. Mural decoration of the exedra in the 'House of the Coloured Stuccos', Pella. Pella Museum. Late 3rd century BC.

Fig. 40. Cup. Foundry scene. Berlin, Staatl. Museen. About 490-480 BC.

of this decoration; domestic rooms were not 'homely' or 'snug' in form, a point to which we shall return.

Allusions to architectural features of public buildings were not the only means of enriching the repertoire of domestic mural decoration. Small relief figures in applied stucco are also encountered, such as masks of Medusa, satyrs or warriors[37] (see cover ill.). None has been found in its original position, but they were obviously placed above the string course, giving the impression that they were hanging on the wall, just like free-modelled terracottas (fig. 53).

The practice of hanging various objects on the walls was certainly an old one and is frequently seen in vase-paintings. In a foundry scene (fig. 40), the relief masks and *pinakes* (painted pictures)[38] on the wall have a cult character, and the same applies to similar works in domestic rooms. When the *androns* acquired mural decoration in the late fifth century BC, this practice was not abandoned. Free-modelled terracottas and reliefs occurred, such as fig. 53 and the masks mentioned above (see cover ill.), which virtually abolish the dividing line between mural decoration and sculpture; anyway, as we have seen, the mural decoration could also include architectural sculptures[39].

So we can establish that the figural element existed both as painting and as relief in mural decorations, that is in this element too colour and modelling carried equal weight. Moreover, the relief figures are very small, like the painted friezes (figs 30,32). In other words, the figural element, whether painted or in relief, visually played a minor role in the decoration as a whole.

Small pictures like those in the foundry scene fig. 40, were also hung on the walls. Such *pinakes* were frequently dedicated in sanctuaries (note 38) and had a votive character in the house too. A letter has survived of one Theophilos, an Alexandrian painter of the first half of the third century BC, to a client, whom he asks to order *pinakes* from him. Theophilos was not an artist of stature, rather he was a skilful artisan who also executed parts (the most important) of mural decorations in houses[40].

This art of mural decoration, fully developed by the latest in the early fourth century BC, subsequently spread, like the

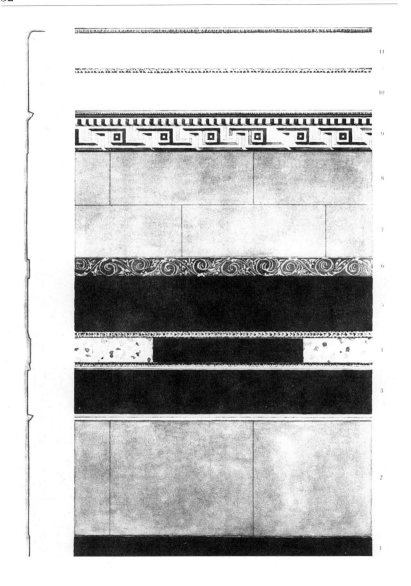

Fig. 41. Panticapaeum (Kerch). Mural decoration of a house. St. Petersburg, Hermitage. Hellenistic period.

Fig. 42. Detail of fig. 41.

peristyle court, throughout the Hellenistic world. Though
regional groups with certain specific traits existed, the
underlying morphological principle discussed above was
common to all. It obtained, for example, in the houses at
Panticapaeum (fig. 41-42)[41], even though the structure of the
wall – the various mouldings and ornamental zones on the
upper part interrupting the courses – reveals the efforts of a
local workshop. Evidently the original concept and intention of
this decoration were not so clearly understood in the periphery
of the Hellenic world.

The so-called First Pompeian style is another local style,
within the Late Hellenistic *koine* of mural decoration[42].
Though here the sense of wall structure is not as weak as in the
Crimea (fig. 41-42), it is nevertheless less developed than in
mainland Greece (figs 27,30,32,33).

What of the *ceiling* decoration in the rooms with such walls?

This is an issue about which almost nothing is known. No
decorated ceiling has been found in excavation, or at least none
has been published[43]. Nor can we consider the ceiling decoration in Macedonian tombs as an argument in favour of its
existence in houses, since the decorative principles of the tombs
differ from those of houses (see note 31). There is, however,
indirect evidence. We learn from the letter of the painter
Theophilos (note 40) that in the houses of Ptolemaic Egypt, in
the first half of the third century BC, decorated ceilings were
not unusual. And earlier in Athens, it is noteworthy that Plato
explicitly mentions 'ceiling decorations' (*Politeia* 529B). So it
seems that when mural decoration was created the ceiling was
not neglected; it was probably decorated with applied stucco

43. Delos, 'House of Dionysos', room D. Fragment of mural decoration: pillared portico in the upper storey with coffering drawn in perspective. Late 2nd cent. BC. Delos Museum.

coffers, imitating the coffered ceilings in public buildings such as the Hieron on Samothrace (fig. 36)[44]. In other words, the decoration of the ceiling, like that of the walls, visually assimilated the domestic interior to the public one; the consistency in reference to public buildings is significant.

It would appear, therefore, that at the end of the fifth century BC yet another 'ennobling domestic art' was born: the decorated ceiling.

Mosaics

We know much more about *floors*, because mosaics are often the only evidence of an *andron* found in excavation.

Pebble floors existed in Greece in earlier times, but mosaic pictures only appeared in public buildings and private houses at

Fig. 44. Eretria, 'La maison aux mosaïques' (fig. 6). Andron 8 and 9.

art in the fourth century BC: colour grading gives the floral forms a sculptural quality and shading on the volutes imparts a spatial dimension. The '*ἄνθινα ἐδάφη*' ('flowery floors') in the house of Demetrios Phalereus in Athens must have been similar mosaics[50].

Ornaments are one of the main themes in fourth-century BC mosaics. Others are gods, such as Dionysos (fig. 51), mythological scenes (such as Theseus raping Helen [fig. 11], Amazonomachy [fig. 11], Arimasps fighting griffins [fig. 45], Heracles against a centaur and Bellerophon against the

Fig. 49. Mosaic from an andron at Sicyon. Sicyon Museum. About 360-350 BC.

Chimaera, Nereids bearing weapons to Achilles etc.), mythological creatures (gorgoneia [fig. 46], centaurs etc.; sea creatures are particularly common); hunting scenes (fig. 11,50);
animal friezes and groups of fighting animals (figs 48,52)[51]. The
repertoire is rich; the mosaic masters moved freely in the world
of imagery of the time, and so there are numerous parallels
with works in other arts, some of which, such as painted clay
vases, were also to be found in houses. There was no
programme dictating the choice of subject – this is also true of
the painted friezes in the mural decorations (figs 30,32)[52].

It is significant that the subjects of the mosaics as a rule
bore no relationship to the function of the rooms to which they
belonged. Moreover, we cannot deduce from the theme whether
a mosaic comes from a house or a public building; there was in

*Fig. 50. Mosaic from the 'House of Dionysos' (fig. 8, no 1,10). Pella Museum.
About 330-320 BC.*

Fig. 51. Mosaic from the 'House of Dionysos' (fig. 8, no 1,10). Pella Museum. About 330-320 BC.

Fig. 52. Threshold mosaic from the 'House of Dionysos' (fig. 8, no 1,10). Pella Museum. About 330-320 BC.

fact no 'domestic iconography'. The mosaic pictures did not embody domestic values, nor did they refer to the houseowner in any way; they gave no indication of his profession, personality, personal preferences... The same holds for the whole furbishing of domestic space. And yet free as they are from programme, personal allusions or symbolism, the mosaics enable us to understand something of the singularity of the new domesticity: through the floor mosaics the large pictures hitherto only found in sanctuaries and public places, entered domestic space and contributed to its new nobility.

Sculpture

The appearance of *marble sculptures* was another contribution to the ennobling of domestic space. Terracottas had always existed in houses, and of course continued to do so after the late fifth century BC; an example is the gorgoneion (fig. 53) which hung on the polychrome walls of the large *andron* in the 'maison aux mosaïques' (fig. 6, no. 7), together with two other masks (of a satyr and a silen) and a snake[53]. By this time, however, marble figures occurred too, such as the statuette of Asclepius, of the mid-fourth century BC, found in the entrance to the *andron* of a house at Olynthos[54]. An early fourth-century BC head from the courtyard of a house at Olynthos perhaps belongs to a herm[55], and the head of a youth (fig. 54), from Eretria, certainly does; the latter stood in the peristyle court of a house[56].

In earlier times herms were set up in sanctuaries, in public places or in the streets beside house doorways (fig. 55)[57]. Well known is the scandal of the mutilation of the herms, when one night during the troubled years of the Peloponnesian War (415 BC) unknown vandals disfigured the faces of almost all the

Fig. 53. Terracotta gorgoneion from andron 7, 'La maison aux mosaïques'
(fig. 6). Eretria Museum. Third quarter of 4th cent. BC.

Fig. 54. Marble head of a boy (herm) from house II at Eretria. Eretria
Museum. About 320 BC.

Fig. 55. Loutrophoros. Wedding procession; in front of the open door of the house, a herm and an altar. Karlsruhe, Badisches Landesmuseum. About 430-420 BC.

Fig. 56. Lekanis lid (detail). Wedding preparations. St. Petersburg, Hermitage. Mid-4th cent. BC.

herms in Athens (Thucydides VI, 27.1), which impiety was attributed to Alcibiades and his cronies. In the fourth century BC herms were also set up in houses; vase-paintings such as fig. 56[58], in which a small herm features in a scene of wedding preparations, give a vivid picture that complements finds such as fig. 54.

Herms inside the house were cult objects as well. In a comedy of the early fourth century BC a polished marble Hermes (herm?) is mentioned as standing beside the *kylikeion*, and before the symposium prayers were addressed to the god[59].

It must have been a statuette (or a small herm); as a rule not only the terracottas but also the marble figures were considerably smaller than life-size; domestic cult was simple.

A common rite was the crowning of the herm with a wreath – Theophrastos' *Deisidaimon* (superstitious one) performed this quite regularly in his house (*Charact.* 16, 10). It was also usual for feasters leaving a symposium to crown the herm with the wreath they had worn during it. This custom is mentioned in a story showing the sagacity (σωφροσύνη) of the philosopher Xenocrates: around the middle of the fourth century BC he was the guest of the tyrant Dionysos II of Syracuse, and on one occasion he won a wine-drinking contest (Dionysios was very fond of wine!), receiving as a prize a gold wreath; on leaving the banquet the philosopher did not take the wreath with him but placed it on the herm that stood in the courtyard (certainly a peristyle one), thus declaring his indifference to the tyrant's valuable gift[60].

The cult status of the herms in the house is evident, and the same applies to the statuettes of gods, such as the Asclepius from Olynthos (note 54), or even the terracotta figure of Hephaestus set up in the household hearth as 'guardian of the fire'[61]. A statuette of Aphrodite Ourania is mentioned in an epigram of Theocritos (XIII), written as if it were on the base of the work:

'This is not Cypris of the Populace (πάνδαμος). When thou prayest to the goddess name her the Celestial (Οὐρανία), set here by chaste Chrysogona in the house of Amphicles, whose children and whose life she shared. And since with thee, Lady, they made beginning, they have prospered ever from year to year: for those humans that care for the Immortals fare themselves the better'. (Transl. A.S.F. Gow).

Amphicles' wife, being chaste, did not set up in the house a dedication to Aphrodite Pandemos but chose the aspect of the goddess associated with conjugal love and fertility: it was Aphrodite Ourania to whom Chrysogona prayed. At that time Pandemos was mainly the goddess of prostitutes. Theocritos says nothing about the statue's appearance: what mattered to Chrysogona was its *cult value*. As Walter Benjamin pointed out, the reception of works of art (that is the way works of art are understood and function) is each time determined by different values, two of which are diametrically opposite: the cult value (*Kultwert*) and the display value (*Ausstellungswert*)[62]. In the ancient Greek house it was the cult value that was dominant as far as sculpture was concerned, which rules out a decorative (in the later sense) function of sculptures.

Nevertheless, the fact that *marble* sculptures appeared inside the house (marble as a material was characteristic of high art), and that marble herms were found not only in front of the entrance (fig. 55) but also in the house (fig. 56) – in the courtyard and the *androns* – certainly contributed to its new nobility. Now even marble vases and vessels, such as perirrhanteria, were to be found in the house, being used as a rule in domestic cult[63].

However, in sculpture, as in the other arts, there was a limit that was not ignored; no large statues were set up inside the house – in the fourth century BC the statuettes were usually 60-70 cm high, always smaller than life-size.

The cult character of domestic statuary explains why in the

controversy over *tryphe* (luxury), that broke out in Athens in the late fifth century BC, sculpture is not mentioned. The *luxury* condemned by philosophers, orators and comic poets concerned, as is expressly stated in the texts, mural decorations, mosaic floors and splendid textiles.

Textiles

It is not unintentional that Plato stresses in *Protagoras* (see p. 12) that Prodicos was tucked up in blankets and furs: this is in keeping with the caustic, negative characterization of the luxury-loving sophist; the weather was certainly not cold, since the dialogue that followed took place in the courtyard!

Fig. 57. Volute krater, neck detail. Malibu, J. P. Getty Museum. About 400 BC.

Nothing has survived of the sumptuous covers and cushions that were an essential part of the symposium's festive ambience, of the curtains that frequently hung between rooms instead of doors or were draped about the beds. All these are known of only from praise in the literary sources, such as those of the tents of Alcibiades and Dionysios I of Syracuse (see p. 31). Nevertheless, some finds from tombs give us an idea of the quality and variety of textiles, with woven, embroidered or painted designs. The wonderful textile from Vergina comes, of course, from a royal tomb[64], but a linen cloth with silver embroidery (lions in rhomb fields), a fine work of the late fifth century BC, was found in the grave of an Athenian[65]. Greek

Fig. 58. Kalyx krater. Würzburg, Martin v. Wagner Mus. About 400 BC.

Fig. 59. Woollen cover from the sixth tomb of the 'Seven Brothers', with 'red-figure' pictures: zones of patterns and mythological scenes. St. Petersburg, Hermitage. 4th cent. BC.

Fig. 60. Detail of fig. 59.

textiles of the same period or slightly later, from burials in southern Russia, bear ornaments and mythological scenes in polychromy, or even, like the cover figs 59, 60, in 'red-figure' effect[66].

Vase-paintings can also be used as evidence, even though these are not, of course, illustrative in character and can only

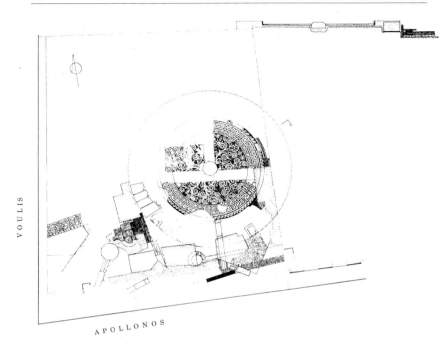

Fig. 61. Athens, Voulis - Apollonos St. Public bath. Mid-4th cent. BC.

give us an inkling of the appearance of the house interior. Nevertheless, these representations, indeed as paintings in their own right, are a contemporary source and – allowing for their peculiar character – a valuable visual aid.

Two Attic vase-paintings : a youth (Adonis?) lying on a couch, surrounded by women (fig. 57)[67], and Dionysos at a

Fig. 62. The mosaic of fig. 61.

symposium together with a young companion, Hephaestus (fig. 58)[68]; two satyrs are the musicians at the feast of the gods. In both representations the splendour of the garments, the couch covers and the cushions is striking, quite unlike the simplicity in the scene of a divine symposium on an Attic cup of about a generation earlier[69].

The Athenians' penchant for luxurious attire in the late fifth century BC is often mentioned in the literary sources: in the satire of Aristophanes, in the censures of Socrates and other philosophers, as well as in the accounts of the appearance of Alcibiades, a key-figure for Athenian society at that time[70].

Another symptom of luxury (*tryphe*) in the late fifth century BC is the rise in the number of public baths (*βαλανεῖα*) in the cities. This did not escape Aristophanes' ridicule, for, unlike the baths for athletes, at Olympia for example, the public baths in the city became meeting places for the Athenian *jeunesse dorée*. Indeed the comic poet points out that they make cowards out of men (*Clouds* 1046ff.) and advises avoidance of them (*Clouds* 991).

A circular room found in Athens seems to belong to a luxurious public bath (fig. 61-62)[71], with a high quality polychrome mosaic of the mid-fourth century BC. In the fifth century BC the public baths had plain mosaic floors, but in the fourth century BC there were baths that apparently rivalled peristyle houses, at least as regards the floor mosaics – nothing else is known of their interior decoration. It was 'noble' public baths such as these that the comic poet Pherecrates (early fourth century BC) surely had in mind when he spoke of the 'youths who take a warm bath early in the morning and are drunk even before the agora fills with people' (2, 29).

Some Athenians were even interested in perfumes and cosmetics, another fashion at which the comic poets poked fun. Callias would have gladly offered his guests oils so that they might enjoy their fragrance, if Socrates had not declined (Xenophon, *Symposium* III 2); indeed in some rich houses there were vases full of aromatic oils (Aristophanes, *Plutos* 810 ff.), and at the banquets of Demetrios Phalereus 'showers of myrrh fell upon the ground', as denounced by Douris of Samos.

Furniture

Among the abundance of written evidence on Athenian society at this time – admonishments and accusations, parody and caricature – there is some that should not be taken literally. Thus, the heated controversy about *tryphe* (which also acquired a political dimension, luxury being associated with an aspiration to tyranny) should not disguise the fact that the houses of wealthy Athenians, which were the target of criticism, were, by our standards, quite simply furnished. There were couches and low tables in the *andrones*, beds, chests, armchairs, chairs and stools in the other rooms ... but nothing that was merely decorative; it is telling, for example, that there

Fig. 63a. Attic pyxis. Wedding preparations (Nereids). London, British Museum. About 435-430 BC.

Fig. 63b-c. Details of fig. 63a.

were no flower vases. Branches, wreaths and garlands were used in the rites of domestic cult, of weddings (fig. 63a-c)[72] and so on. In the floral accoutrements of the symposium cult function and festive decoration went together, and so it is only natural that as the participants left they dedicated their wreath on the herm (see p. 69).

Important information on furniture and household equipment in general, in the late fifth century BC, is provided by the 'Attic stelae' found in the Agora[73]. Recorded on these is the property of Alcibiades and his friends, which was confiscated and auctioned after the trial of the Hermocopids, (see p. 65ff.). The list and the prices evaluated for the furniture and other objects indicate how little sense of luxury (not only by modern standards but by the standards, let us say, of the first century BC) rich Athenians of the late fifth century BC. had – and indeed Alcibiades and his friends, who were notorious for their extravagant life style. Even if we assume that some precious objects had been removed or stolen before the list was compiled[74], this would not apply to the furniture. The fact is that in those days 'there was little sense of personal luxury in Athens'[75].

Costly pieces of furniture did, of course, exist, but these were reserved for the gods and are mentioned as *ex-votos* in the treasury lists of the sanctuaries. What was possible in the first century BC, when Cicero paid an astronomical sum for a table of rare wood, would have been unthinkable in late fifth and fourth-century BC Athens. So, the early peristyle houses were frugally furnished. Moreover, in the domestic interior as a whole the personal touch was hardly felt, or rather was nonexistent. The singular lack of subjectivity which can be clearly seen in the portraits of the period, also determined the character of the house.

In order to understand the creation of the peristyle house and the new interior decoration discussed here, we should take a look at the new *life style* with which this was surely associated. That the much talked about 'need for luxury' led to the peristyle house is hardly a satisfactory explanation, since it immediately raises the question why there was a need for luxury at this time rather than any other. Luxury was not the cause but rather a side issue of the new life style.

Moreover, because the 'noble' house was created as a *special* type of domestic architecture, we should also ask *who* lived in such a manner as to need such a house, and *what* characterized this way of life.

This leads us to the *change in mentality* that took place in the late fifth century BC, mainly in Athens. Even though we cannot prove by excavation that the first peristyle houses were built at Athens – and not for example at Corinth, Sicyon or Eretria – only here is it possible to follow what led to the rise of noble houses in late Classical times.

Apragmosyne and *schole*

The change in mentality attested in Athens in the late fifth century BC, though certainly closely related to political events, represents another aspect of the history of that period. It is, I believe, one of the main features of the phenomenon called as a whole the 'crisis of the polis' (*Poliskrise*).

Let me explain myself. In the turbulent years of the Peloponnesian War and through the radicalization of the Athenian Democracy its very foundations were threatened. People began to doubt even the notion of the *polis*, not to mention certain values which had played a decisive role in society for centuries. Contemporary testimonies indicate diverse, even diametrically opposed, views; in the passionate ideological conflict there were no longer any principles that remained unchallenged.

Telling is the fact that for the first time a fundamental Greek value, *kleos* (fame), was being questioned. Until that time it had been taken for granted that honour and fame should motivate all actions, whether of individual citizens or the *polis* as a whole; now there were men who doubted this. Men who sought instead a quiet life, far from politics and the law courts, who openly expressed their aversion to the hustle and bustle of the Agora.

This change in mentality is borne out by a certain change at this time in the meaning of words such as πολυπραγμοσύνη and its opposites ἀπραγμοσύνη and ἡσυχία[76]. Thucydides praised *polypragmosyne* as the quality that contributed decisively to Athens' greatness in the fifth century BC; the Athenians, leaving neither themselves nor others in peace (πολυπραγ-μονοῦντες), chose laborious activity instead of passivity (ἡσυχία ἀπράγμων) in order to do the right thing (I, 70). Pericles, in his famous funerary oration, called the man who takes no part in public affairs 'not one who minds his own business, but a good for nothing' (Thucydides II, 40, 2). Thucydides stressed that under the leadership of Pericles Athenian '*polypragmosyne*' was combined with 'sagacity' (σωφροσύνη) and so achieved great feats, while after Pericles' death *sophrosyne* was replaced by greed (πλεονεξία), which brought disaster. So the historian valued sagacious *polypragmosyne* as an admirable, creative force and condemned only excesses.

In this same period however, completely different opinions existed, such as that voiced by Ion in the homonymous play by Euripides (first performed in 413 BC). Ion praises contentment without glory (598 ff.): 'The more useful capable sort are wisely silent, and do not seek to meddle in affairs. I shall be laughed at by them if I do not keep quiet in a city full of fear' (Transl. Carter, op. cit. 158).

For Ion, those who sought to opt out of everyday politics

were not 'good for nothing' as Pericles called them, but quite the opposite, honest and capable. For the first time *apragmosyne* is considered an attitude worth striving for.

Ion rejected his father's offer that would bring him fame, power and wealth, preferring instead to remain at Delphi (632 ff.): 'Let me have a moderate portion, so it bring no grief. Let me tell you the great advantage of my life, father; I have leisure (σχολή), man's greatest boon. The people behave with respect to me and do not elbow me aside in the street; if there is one thing I cannot tolerate it is to give way in the street to the low rabble' (Transl. Carter, op. cit. 159).

For Ion *schole* (inadequately translated as 'leisure') was the greatest boon. Thus a new value was born, henceforth to be a main feature of Greek cultural life. This was to have far-reaching consequences.

The word *schole*, as the opposite of ἀσχολία, originally meant 'free time'. In the late fifth century BC, however, the term *schole* acquired an intellectual dimension. Those who cultivated *schole* as a way of life wanted no truck, as Ion says, with the 'low rabble' (that is the demagogues and the commonfolk of Athens led astray by them) and set themselves off not by virtue of their aristocratic origin – or not only by that –, but rather by their life style, characterized by 'leisure' and learning.

Learning is another new value of the age. For the first time, presumably under the influence of the Sophists, people began to buy books; domestic libraries came into being, so that when Aristophanes made fun of Euripides' bookishness (*Frogs* 943.1409) or joked about the affliction of books (*Birds* 974 ff., 1024 ff. 1288), his audience understood and laughed. Significant

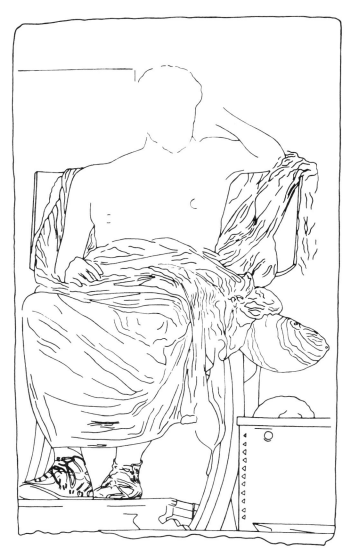

Fig. 64. Funerary naiskos of Hermon, painted portrait of the dead. Hermon sitting in an armchair, near him a bookroll chest with bookroll on top. Athens, Kerameikos Museum. About 340 BC.

for this new tendency is the fact that from now onwards the portrait of the dead on the grave stelae showed him not only in the established types of 'athlete', 'warrior' and so on, but also as a 'man with bookroll' (fig. 64)[77].

Indeed there was no lack of reaction to the new interest in books: Socrates and Plato fought against their dissemination in order to save the oral exchange of views, the dialogue, the *living word*. Their attitude seems strange to us now, as we try to promote books, the written word, in order to protect society from inundation with (moving) pictures. But the situation was quite different then. Early Greek culture was founded mainly on oral speech; as R. Pfeiffer puts it, for the first time in the third century BC, and even then not without reserve, we may speak of a 'reading society'[78].

Apart from this however, *apragmosyne*, as turning away from everyday politics, favoured *schole* as a way of life; *apragmosyne* and *schole* created the conditions for the *contemplative life* that was soon to become Plato's goal[79]. In Euripides' *Antiope* (first performed in 409 BC) the argument between the two brothers Amphion and Zethos presents the two opposite standpoints. Zethos praises the active life and advises his brother: 'listen to me and stop singing; concern yourself instead with the muse of War. Those should be your songs and you'll be known as a sensible man digging and ploughing the earth and tending the flocks, leaving the elegant sophistries to others, for these will make you live in an empty house' (fr. 188).

He speaks for those Athenians who dismiss the Sophists, and Socrates too, as 'hairsplitters'.

Amphion, however, is a determined *apragmon*, pointing out

that: 'Whoever meddles in many things, without being obliged to do so, is a fool; whereas he might live free of care as *apragmon*' (fr. 193). And he stresses: 'If a man is prosperous, and enjoying a good life, and does not cultivate things of beauty (*kala*) at home, I should not call him fortunate, just the guardian of his wealth' (fr. 198; transl. Carter, op. cit. 168).

Ta kala is one of those ancient Greek words whose full meaning is difficult to convey by just one word: '*μηδὲν τῶν καλῶν πειράσεται*' means 'he cultivates not only beautiful but also good things': this of course includes merry-making and drinking, but also pondering and discussing scientific and philosophical matters, as well as issues of political theory.

The *schole* that Ion and Amphion sought above all led to the *schole* in which the Platonic dialogues are conducted: 'There is the following difference between slaves and free men... The free man always has time at his disposal to converse in peace at his leisure... the others are slaves' (Plato, *Theaitetos* 172d).

Turning away from everyday politics was not a form of escapism – to nature or to an unworldly domestic realm. The *apragmones* were city-dwellers and politics were part of their thoughts and discussions – after all the peristyle houses were city houses not rural retreats. Socrates was not just speaking for himself when he frankly declared that nature held no interest for him: 'You see I am fond of learning. Now the country places and the trees won't teach me anything, whereas the people in the city do' (Plato, *Phaidros* 230D).

Characteristic of the change in mentality in the late fifth century BC is Aristophanes' change in his attitude towards Athens[80]. In the early comedies the poet dealt with current politics: he satirized Athens' evils, traduced the demagogue

Cleon or certain citizens – whose greed was leading the city to disaster, parodied the Athenians' passion for trials and law-courts and inveighed against such modernisms as self-serving discussions, (*sophisteies*) that were potentially damaging to the young; he expressed the Athenians' desire for peace at last, and all in all attacked certain ills so that the city might regain its former glory.

In the troubled years following Nicias' peace (421 BC), the issues changed, and so did the poet's targets. Aristophanes continued to tackle current concerns – he spoke out against Alcibiades, satirizing his vanity and ostentatious life style – but in *Birds* (414 BC) he was clearly a weary man: he no longer attacked particular persons or events, to him the haplesness was total. There appear in the play two Athenian citizens who, heartily sick of the passion for litigation in the city, leave it in search of a peaceful land (characteristically: τόπον ἀπράγμονα [*Birds* 4]). They find it in the clouds and there set up a state of birds – a fairytale world (cloud-cuckoo-land) is thus projected as an opposite image of Athenian *polypragmosyne*. Here Aristophanes expressed his weariness with daily politics as well as his tendency to invent political theories, even if these are presented as delightful caricature.

In *Frogs* too (405 BC) the action no longer takes place in Athens. Aristophanes sets his criticism of tragedy in the Underworld and the subject is of a theoretical nature; it can of course be considered political in the wider sense, but it does not allude to current events.

In his later works (*Ekklesiazousai*, 392 BC; *Plutus*, 388 BC) Aristophanes devised only social and economic theories, such as that of communal ownership of women and property...

Such a development is not only characteristic of Aristophanes. In Athens at this time, wider circles began to discuss the fundamental principles of politics; much was also put down in writing – and the fourth century BC became the golden age of Greek prose. It is probably Plato who most assiduously combined a *contemplative life (βίος θεωρητικὸς)* with participation in politics[81]. He tried twice (366-365 BC, 361-360 BC) to educate a sovereign! And he surely failed. What is significant, however, is not just that he tried but that Dionysios II of Syracuse had insisted on having him as counsellor and mentor. Not long afterwards, Philip II of Macedon managed to bring another famous philosopher from Athens to teach his son and heir; Aristotle became tutor to Alexander.

To recall such events is not to digress from the question why a noble house type was created in these years. They were all related to the new way of life – that aimed at *apragmosyne*, as detachment from politics, and regarded *schole* as the ultimate value. The Athenian *schole*, where discussions on science, philosophy, political theory or art took place became an impetus which made Athens the centre of Greece in the fourth century BC: a centre not of political power but of culture.

The house appropriate to this new way of life was the type created at this time: the peristyle house with the interior features described above. Such a house provided, as it were, a suitable setting for those wishing 'to cultivate things of beauty and excellence at home' (p. 89) – architecture and lifestyle were mutually determined.

A side issue of the new life style was the *public character emulated in domestic space*:

Up until the late fifth century BC there was a marked distinction between the *oikos* (house, family) and the *polis* (the public sector, mainly the domain of political activity, since economic affairs were the province of the *oikos*)[82]. This distinction also concerned the different roles of the two genders: the *oikos* was primarily the responsibility of women, public affairs were conducted by men. Hector's encounter with Andromache in Book Z´ of the *Iliad* clearly presents the male-female polarity: Andromache represents the values of the *oikos*, caring for home and child, without of course doubting the values of men, which would lead Hector to war and perhaps to death. In the years when the peristyle house was born, male values, in a way, invaded the home: brought by the men who began to question these selfsame values or to weigh them up, scrutinizing their underlying principles. Because discussion of these matters took place not in the Agora but in the house, the domestic interior was given a visually public character: with the colonnades, mural decorations, mosaic floors and so on[83].

The *public character of the domestic interior* is, therefore, a symptom of the singular nature of *schole* in the late fifth and the fourth century BC. *Schole* was the central value of the new lifestyle in the peristyle house.

Heracleides Criticos, a travel-writer of the late (?) third century BC, noted after visiting Athens (*On the Cities in Greece* I, 1): 'The city is all dry, without having a good water supply; as it was built long ago it is badly laid out. Most of the houses are humble, very few reach a higher standard'. Athens was indeed an old city, with no Hippodamian town plan, and the density of habitation made the building of splendid houses difficult (see p. 21 ff.).

However, Heracleides' remarks are also a rhetorical device, in order to emphasize what he says next. He continues: 'At first sight a stranger will find it hard to believe that this is the famous city called Athens. Soon, however, he will believe it. Here there are the most beautiful things in the world: a notable theatre, large and impressive; a splendid sanctuary of Athena, far from the noise of the city, a sight to behold; above the theatre the so-called Parthenon makes a great impression on pilgrims; the Olympieum, which, though half finished, is impressively designed; it would be superb if it were completed; three Gymnasia, the Academy, the Lyceum, the Cynosarges, all full of trees and lawns. [Here are held] all sorts of festivities, recreation of the spirit is offered by all kinds of philosophers; [there are] many study and discussion groups, and continuous contemplation'[84].

For Heracleides the theatre, the temples, the philosophers' *gymnasia* and groves, and whatever took place within them, constituted Athens. He recorded thus what the city meant to him and his contemporaries. The festivities, the philosophers' schools, the discussions and the practice of the *contemplative life* – here is described the noble *schole* lifestyle, which one could experience in Athens more than anywhere else.

The houses of the wealthy Athenians were, like the philosophers' groves, places where one practised *schole*. Indeed the noble houses existed before the founding of the philosophical schools. Let us end by looking at an Athenian house, which can be justifiably considered as one of the first peristyle houses, even though it is known only from the literary sources: the house of Callias in the aristocratic quarter of Melite. This was the house chosen by Plato as the venue for his dialogue *Protagoras*; Xenophon's *Symposium* took place in a second house belonging to Callias, in Piraeus; for the Athenian house at least a peristyle court is explicitly mentioned (see p. 11f.). Of course I do not claim that this house, legendary because of the Platonic dialogue, is the earliest peristyle house in antiquity, but that its owner – who was the target of criticism and persiflage by the comic poets of the day, yet also had a good name and was well liked – can be considered a key-person for the lifestyle discussed above.

Callias was the scion of an old family of priests at Eleusis and was himself initiated in the Mysteries; he also continued family tradition as a victor in the games at Delphi, Nemea and Isthmus, and as such dedicated a four-horse chariot in the sanctuary at Delphi[85]. His mother had married Pericles in a second marriage, his sister was the (unfortunate) wife of Alcibiades; so Callias was one of the noblest men in Athens. He inherited a large fortune from his father (who died shortly before 421 BC) and kept an open house: his generosity to the Sophists was unrivalled and, as Plato records (p. 11 ff.), he entertained the most famous. On the other hand he was a great admirer of Socrates; in Xenophon's *Symposium*, Callias insists that Socrates and his friends attend the dinner he is giving to celebrate the athletic victory of the handsome youth Autolycos. Eminent men were not his only guests, there were hangers-on too, who took advantage of him, as Eupolis lampooned in his comedies *The Flatterers* and *Autolycos*... Callias was a bon viveur, fond of drink and love-making – but he also had an agile mind and was avid of learning. He promoted discussion in his house not only by offering the ambience and spending money, but also by his urbane qualities.

He was one of those men who, being a good listener, create the conditions conducive to genuine discussion. European history has witnessed paramount moments of dialogue, and of *schole*, when masterpieces of art were born. The earliest highspot of this kind, a lifestyle that cultivated dialogue, was the *schole* of the Athenians in the late fifth and the fourth century BC. And there existed too the genius Plato, who elevated dialogue to a philosophy, with far-reaching consequences for contemporary and later thought.

Through the *schole* of the Athenians the peristyle house was born, as the house of a higher lifestyle. When the young Cicero visited Athens it was the legendary centre not only of learning and philosophy, but also of a superior way of life as a whole. Isocrates had acknowledged this role for Athens already in 380 BC (*Panegyric*), and his were no empty words. The remarkable diffusion of this new type of domestic architecture was undeniably related to the leading cultural role of Athens. Peristyle houses were built all over Greece, and then throughout the Hellenistic world, for the new Athenian way of life became the model, at least for a certain social class, in the Hellenistic cities. The mentality as well as the type of house were adopted, imitated and locally varied, then in the course of time transformed into something new.

So the *schole* of the Athenians in Late Classical times was the stimulus for the rise of noble houses.

Abbreviations

The abbreviations are those used by the Archaeological Society, plus:

ANDREOU   A. ANDREOU, *Griechische Wanddekorationen* (Diss. Mainz 1988)

ANDRONIKOS   M. ANDRONIKOS, *Vergina. The Royal Tombs and the Ancient City* (1984)

BULARD   M. BULARD, *MonPiot* XIV, 1908

HOEPFNER-SCHWANDNER   W. HOEPFNER - E.L. SCHWANDNER, *Haus und Stadt im klassischen Griechenland* (Wohnen in der klassischen Polis I) 1986

LAUTER   H. LAUTER, *Die Architektur des Hellenismus* (1986)

SALZMANN   D. SALZMANN, *Untersuchungen zu den antiken Kieselmosaiken* (1982)

TRAVLOS   J. TRAVLOS, *Bildlexikon zur Topographie des antiken Athen* (1971)

Notes

1. The *liturgies* are known of in detail, primarily from Athens, and it is characteristic that they still existed in the fourth century BC, even though they had lost much of their former status; there were by then measures to protect the *liturgoi*; there were, for instance, citizens who 'camouflaged' their wealth in order to avoid the obligation... All these measures required greater expenditure on administration and it is thus hardly surprising that the *liturgies* were abolished by Demetrios Phalereus in the late fourth century BC (cf. S. LAUFFER, Die Liturgien in der Krisenperiode Athens in E. Ch. WELSKOPF (ed., *Hellenische Poleis* I, 1974, 147 f. M.I. FINLEY, *Politics in the Ancient World* [1983] 24 ff. M. AUSTIN - P. VIDAL-NAQUET, *Gesellschaft und Wirtschaft im alten Griechenland* (1984) 100 ff.).

2. Cf. HOEPFNER - SCHWANDNER 270. That one of these elements may be missing – e.g. a peristyle house might have mural decorations but not mosaics (cf. PH. BRUNEAU, *Archeologia* 27, 1976, 25 f.) does not change the fact of their emergence at the same time, which raises the question: What is the common meaning?

3. Cf. W. HOEPFNER, Das Pompeion (*Kerameikos* X, 1976) 129-130. We do not refer here to isolated precursors, such as the peristyle court in the *hestiatorion* of the Keans on Delos, about 480/470 BC (CHR. BÖRKER, Festbankett und griechische Architektur [*Xenia* 4, 1983] 16 ff. fig. 11).

4. On 'la maison aux mosaïques' see P. DUCREY-I. METZGER, *AntK* 22, 1979, 3 ff. K. REBER, *AA* 1988, 653 ff. ibidem *AntK* 32, 1989, 3 ff. P. DUCREY-I. METZGER-K. REBER, Le quartier de la maison aux mosaïques, (*Eretria* VIII, 1993).

5. Cf. M. JAMESON, Private Space and the Greek City, in O. MURRAY-S. PRICE (eds.), *The Greek City from Homer to Alexander* (1990) 191.

6. Cf. M. KREEB, *AA* 1985, 95 ff. fig. 2.8. J. RAEDER, *Gymnasium* 95,

1988, 342 ff. In the 'House of the Masks' the peristyle court is enhanced with a pictorial floor mosaic as was customary in the second century BC.

7. Cf. M. CARROLL - SPILLECKE, *ΚΗΠΟΣ, der antike griechische Garten* (1989) 49 ff., 60 f.

8. CH. MAKARONAS - E. YOURI, *Οἱ οἰκίες ἁρπαγῆς τῆς Ἑλένης καὶ Διο-νύσου* (1989). Plan of the 'House of Dionysos': idem. 153 fig. 142; a different plan: LAUTER fig. 45a. In my opinion LAUTER reconstructed the entrance correctly, because the reconstruction with two columns placed exactly at the point of entry (fig. 10) gives a propylon form unconvincing for a private house; in any case only a fragment of column was found there, and not *in situ*. Date: note 14.

9. Rape of Helen mosaic: SALZMANN, no. 101 pl. 35. MAKARONAS - YOURI, op. cit. 164. Stag hunt mosaic: SALZMANN no. 103 pl. 29, col. pls 101, 2.6, 102, 1-2. MAKARONAS - YOURI, op. cit. 165-166. Amazonomachy mosaic: SALZMANN no. 104 pl. 32 f. MAKARONAS - YOURI, op. cit. 166-167. Cf. note 14.

10. HOEPFNER - SCHWANDNER 108 ff. fig. 104, 1.123.266. S. DAKARIS in *Ὁ ὁμηρικὸς οἶκος* (*Proceedings V Conf. on the Odyssey* [1987] 1990) 206 ff. fig. 4 ff.

11. Cf. H. DRERUP, *RM* 66, 1959, 147 ff. H. MIELSCH, *Die römische Villa* (1987) 139 ff. and passim.

12. In ATHENAEUS, *Deipnos*. XII 542D.

13. SALZMANN no. 96 pl. 34. MAKARONAS - YOURI, op. cit. 133 ff.

14. SALZMANN no. 98 pls 30-31. MAKARONAS - YOURI op. cit. 137 ff., 167 f. The mosaics in both houses (figs 8,1 and 5.9-11) are contemporary with the building of the houses. D. SALZMANN dates the mosaics to 340/330-320/310 BC, D. WILLERS (*HASB* 5, 1979, 23-24) to 340-320 BC. On the dating about 330-320 BC see E. WALTER-KARYDI in *AncMaced* (5th Int. Symp., 1989 [1993] 1732 ff.).

15. H.P. ISLER, *AntK* 22, 1979, 65 ff. The parapets of the upper storey are decorated (ibidem 70; the decoration has not been rendered in fig. 15). Idem. *AntK* 34, 1991, 69 ff.: about 300 BC. K. DALCHER, *Das Peristylhaus I von Iaitas* (*Studia Ietina* VI, 1994).

16. O. ALEXANDRI, *AD* 22, 1967, Chron. 98 ff. pl. 91 ff.; ibidem 30, 1975, B1, 24 ff. fig. 5 pl. 25b. J.W. GRAHAM, *Phoenix* 28, 1974, 52 f. fig. 3: early fourth century BC. CHR. BÖRKER, *ZPE* 29, 1978, 45 n. 15: mosaics earlier than those of Pella. SALZMANN no. 21.22 pl. 42.43: about 310-300 BC. The house can be dated only on the basis of the mosaics. That these

are of the early fourth century BC is indicated by the flat rendering of the designs, the coloration, without shading, and finally the composition of the anteroom mosaic, with concentric friezes around a small central motif and animal groups in the corners (cf. p. 58). J.E. JONES, Town and Country Houses of Attica in Classical Times, in *Misc. Graeca* I, 1975, 96 fig. 10, 1.

17. Cf. *Histor. Stadtplan von Athen* (1989) D4 (the city wall is not preserved at this point and has been restored on the plan).

18. I. THREPSIADIS, *AD* 16, 1960, Chron. 29 ff. pls 30-31. JONES, op. cit. 93 fig. 9. Cf. *Histor. Stadtplan* op. cit. D4.

19. R. YOUNG, An Industrial District of Ancient Athens (*Hesperia* 20, 1951, 135-288). The houses fig. 1 belong here too.

20. H. v. HESBERG in *Bathron* (*Festschr. H. Drerup*, 1988) 186. M. KREEB, *Untersuchungen zur figürl. Ausstattung delischer Privathäuser* (Diss. 1988) 81 f.

21. There are differences between the reconstruction by D. Pandermalis (fig. 20.21) and that by J. Travlos (ANDRONIKOS fig. 18), concerning the east side of the building too; the final publication is still awaited. Cf. also LAUTER 152 ff. 204 f. 234 ff.

22. M. SIGANIDOU, *AEMTH* 1, 1987 (1988) 119 ff; ibidem 2, 1988 (1991) 101 ff.; ibidem 3, 1989 (1992) 59 ff. B. MISAILIDOU - DESPOTIDOU ibidem 67 ff. The estimated area of the palace is 60,000 m²!

23. H.V. HERRMANN, *Olympia* (1972) 170. V. HEERMANN, *AM* 99, 1984, 243 ff.

24. R. SEAGER, Alcibiades and the charge of aiming at tyranny (*Historia* 16, 1967, 6 ff., especially 8 ff.). On the pilgrims' lodgings see recently M. DILLON, The house of the Thebans (*FD* III 1,357-358) and acommodation for Greek pilgrims (*ZPE* 83, 1990, 64 ff.).

25. W. HOEPFNER suggests (*Kerameikos* X, 1976, 103 f.) that the mural decorations figs. 27 and 33 are from a renovation of the banqueting halls of the Pompeium (figs 3.4); they can, however, be used as examples for domestic *andrones* too. Mural decorations of the fourth century BC: from Athens (V. BRUNO, *AJA* 73, 1969, 306 pl. 69 figs 8-10), from Olynthos (ANDREOU cat. nos 144-146 and especially 147), from Eretria, 'la maison aux mosaïques' fig. 6 (*Eretria* VIII [note 4] 36), from Pella, houses fig. 9.10 (MAKARONAS - YOURI op. cit. 145) etc.

26. Cf. recently R. TOMLINSON, *BSA* 85, 1990, 405 ff. J. Travlos's reconstruction has been doubted by J. DE WAELE, *The Propylaia of the*

Acropolis in Athens (1990) 30 ff. V. BRUNO (op. cit. 316 ff.) had already pointed to the monumental architecture of Athens in the late fifth century BC as the model for domestic mural decorations; in my opinion, the temples should be excluded; the aim was assimilation to public buildings for assembly.

27. Fig. 30: ANDREOU cat. no. 92 with bibl. Fig. 32: ibidem cat. no. 107 with bibl. An earlier example: the string-course frieze from a house in Rhodes (GR. KONSTANTINOPOULOS, *AAA* 6, 1973, 123 f. figs 11-12: third century BC at the latest. Idem, Ἀρχαία Ῥόδος [1986] col. pl. 30).

28. PAUSANIAS 1, 22, 6-8. Cf. DÖRPFELD, *AM* 36, 1911, 52 ff., 92 ff. *Pinakes* are mentioned in the texts also for other such buildings in sanctuaries, e.g. on Kynthos on Delos: *Inscr. Délos* 1403 Bb II 29.33 (about 166-156/55 BC); 1417 A47-58 (about 156/55 BC).

29. PSEUDO-ANDOC., *Against Alcibiades* 17. DEMOSTHENES, *Against Meidias* (XXI) 147 (Schol.: OVERBECK, *SQ* 1125). PLUTARCH, *Alcibiades* 16, 5. Cf. SEAGER op. cit. (note 24). Only rarely and by chance is the name of a painter who executed domestic mural decorations recorded (p. 51).

30. ANDRONIKOS 86 ff. fig. 46 ff. Idem *AE* 1987, 371 ff. pl. 2 (preliminary sketch).

31. The arrangement of the decoration inside the Macedonian tombs does not of course always conform to the rules applying to domestic decorations; thus in trying to sort out typological groups of decoration, tomb chambers should be distinguished from domestic rooms.

32. *AvP* VI, 47 ff. Cf. W. RADT, *Pergamon* (1988) 91-92 (Baugruppe IV).

33. E.g. from Delos, with relief rosettes and bucrania (J. MARCADÉ, *BCH* 76, 1952, 110 fig. 9a.b), with bulls' heads (ibidem fig. 9c), with painted representations (BULARD 153-154 pl. VIIIb). Triglyphs and metopes are usually polychrome, indeed following the colour canon of monumental architecture (cf. e.g. fig. 43).

34. A. LAIDLAW, *The First Style in Pompeii* (1985) pl. 97c (casa I. 15.1/3). G. IRELLI - M. AOYAGI - ST. DE CARO - M. PAPPALARDO (eds.), *Pompeianische Wandmalerei* (1990) col. pl. 36.

35. The dating of the interior decoration of the Hieron (fig. 36) to the second half of the fourth century BC by PH. W. LEHMANN (*Samothrace* III [1969] 142, 208-212) has been doubted (cf. recently P. GULDAGER BILDE, The International Style: Aspects of Pompeian First Style and its eastern

equivalents, in *Aspects of Hellenism in Italy* (*ActaHyperb* 5, [1993] 157).
However, in my opinion, this doubt is due to our poor knowledge of
fourth-century BC mural decorations and overlooks the fact that in
outstanding peristyle houses in this century, such as figs 8, no.
1 and 5, figs 9,10,18,19, the mural decorations will have been of particularly high
quality, with elements such as the mini-colonnades. To the examples
from fourth-century BC houses (note 25) the mural decorations in the
palace at Vergina should be added (M. ANDRONIKOS - CH. MAKARONAS -
N. MOUTSOPOULOS - G. BAKALAKIS, Tὸ ἀνάκτορο τῆς Βεργίνας [1961] 27-
28). Noteworthy too is the small tholos in the Cabeirion on Samothrace,
which J. McCREDIE rightly dates to the second half of the fourth century
BC, characterizing it as an antecedent of the Arsinoeum (*Samothrace* 7
[1992] 262 ff. pls 79-92). The reconstruction of the exterior (ibidem pl.
92) not only shows what morphological enhancement was achieved in
the Arsinoeum (figs 37,38), but also what a kindred form this is to the
mural decorations in the Hieron (fig. 36) thus supporting the view that
these are about contemporary to the tholos. In any case, such a 'two-
storey' arrangement was not unusual at the time.

36. On the house see M. SIGANIDOU, Ἀρχαιολογία 2, Feb. 1982, 33ff.
Plan: ibidem fig. 3. In a personal communication (December 1992), the
excavator informed me that the house is dated to the late third century
BC. I warmly thank her for permission to publish the photograph fig. 39.
The walls in room D of the 'house of Dionysos' on Delos (ANDREOU cat.
no. 104 with bibl.) had similar decoration (late second century BC), but
the surviving fragment of the pillared portico (fig. 43: BULARD pl. VIII A,
k) does not show whether there were parapets between the pillars here
and what was the colour of the fields below the roof coffering which is
rendered in perspective.

37. From Delos: J. MARCADÉ, *BCH* 76, 1952, 111 fig. 10 (colour:
BULARD 153 pl. VIII A, i.j.l.m); from Priene: J. RAEDER, *Priene* (1984) cat.
no. 354 fig. 7b. M. BULARD had already rejected the assumption that such
masks belonged to relief metopes.

38. *Pinakes* are mentioned in the 'Attic stelae' (W. PRITCHETT,
Hesperia 25, 1956, 250-253). On the 'Attic stelae' see p. 82. Types of
pinakes in the Delos inscriptions: R. VALLOIS, *Mél. Holleaux* (1913) 37ff.
Cf. here note 28.

39. P. 45 note 33. Cf. also bull protomes from houses at Erythrae (O.
BINGÖL, *AA* 1988, 511 ff. 14-16. ANDREOU 220-221) and on Delos

(MARCADÉ op. cit. fig. 9d. BULARD fig. 52e). Cf. H. V. HESBERG, *RM* 24, Ergh. (1980) 60 ff.

40. M. NOWICKA in *Alexandria e il mondo ellenistico-romano (Studi in onore di A. Adriani*, 1984) 256 ff. 259.

41. ANDREOU cet. no. 174. A mural decoration from a house at Phanagoria is very similar (ibidem cat. no. 173). I have not mentioned the controversy concerning the characterization of Hellenistic mural decoration as 'Architectural style', 'Masonry style', 'Zone style' and so on, because this has nothing to do with the process of ennobling the domestic interior, that is the subject in hand.

42. See recently: LAIDLAW (note 34); idem in *Pompeianische Wandmalerei* (note 34) 205 ff. R. A. TYBOUT, *Aedificiorum figurae* (1989) 109 ff. R. LING, *Roman Painting* (1991) 12 ff. P. GULDAGER BILDE, who has recently studied the Hellenistic mural decorations found in Italy outside Pompeii, points out that these are distinct from the Pompeian ones and indeed more 'Hellenizing' (op. cit. [note 35] 151 ff). If this is true (P. GULDAGER BILDE is going to publish these non-Pompeian decorations), then the 'First Pompeian Style' is just one of the regional groups in Italy.

43. A stucco fragment from Priene, at first thought to be a ceiling coffer, is considered by F. WARTKE as part of a mural decoration *(Forschungen und Berichte* 18, 1977, 34-35 cat. nos 19-20 pl. 7, 1). Cf. R. LING, *BSR* 40, 1972, 40. Idem *Roman Painting* (1991) 18.

44. Ceiling of the Hieron: *Samothrace* III (1969) 142 ff fig. 94.

45. Cf. PH. BRUNEAU, *Archeologia* 27, 1976, 16 ff.

46. Fig. 48: SALZMANN no. 117 pl. 22, 1.

47. 'Dionysos House' (SALZMANN nos 94, 99 pls 37, 1.2. MAKARONAS - YOURI op. cit. fig. 138 f.).

48. SALZMANN no. 118 pls 20-21.101, 1: about 360-350 BC. F. CILIBERTO, *HASB* 14, 1991, 11 ff. (with too low a date).

49. SALZMANN no. 130 pls 39-40. ANDRONIKOS fig. 19.20.

50. Douris of Samos (ATHENAEUS, *Deipnos.* XII 542): ἄνθινά τε πολλὰ ἐκ τῶν ἐδαφῶν ἐν τοῖς ἀνδρῶσι κατεσκευάζετο διαπεποικιλμένα ὑπὸ δημιουργῶν. These 'floors' have always been interpreted as mosaics; a different opinion: CHR. BÖRKER (*ZPE* 29, 1978, 43 ff. with bibl.) and SALZMANN 10. An example of a 'flowery floor' from Athens is the mosaic of a public bath (figs 61-62).

51. Fig. 61-62: SALZMANN no. 95 pl. 36; ibidem other examples of various subjects.

52. Cf. I. BALDASSARE, *DArch* 2, 1984, 71 ff. On the Late Hellenistic houses of Delos: U. T. BEZERRA DE MENESES, *Quaderni DdArch*, 1985 (Ricerche di pittura ellenist.) 215 ff. KREEB op. cit. (note 20) 83 ff.

53. I. METZGER, *Eretria* VIII (note 4) 118 figs 185-188.

54. *Olynthus* XII (1946) 130 ff. pls 115 f., 118 f.

55. *Olynthus* II (1930) 74 ff. figs 195-197. *Olynthus* XII (1946) 130 note 66. E. HARRISON, *Agora* XI (1965) 128-129, 161 pl. 67b.

56. J. M. GARD, *AntK* 17, 1974, 50 ff. pl. 11 ff.

57. K. SCHEFOLD, *Jdl* 52, 1937, 55 ff. figs 14-17. *CVA* Karlsruhe 3 pl. 44 f. inserted pl. 2 (C. WEISS). J. H. OAKLEY-R. H. SINOS, *The Wedding in Ancient Athens* (1993) figs 16-19.

58. SCHEFOLD op. cit. 56 note 5. P. VALAVANIS, *Panathenaic amphoras from Eretria* (1991) 282 ff. pl. 126. OAKLEY-SINOS op. cit. figs 44-45.

59. Ἑρμῆς ὁ Μαίας λίθινος, ὃν προσεύγμασιν ἐν τῷ κυλικείῳ λαμπρὸν ἐκτετριμμένον (frgt. by EUBOULOS in ATHENAEUS *Deipnos.* XI 460e). On the *kylikeion* see G. RICHTER, *Furniture* (1966) 81 ff. fig. p. 83. Cf. also Theopompos on the god-fearing Clearchos who in his home used to wreath and polish Hermes and Hecate; the polishing indicates that the figures of the gods were of marble (in PORPHYRIOS, *De abstinentia* II, 16).

60. TIMAIOS in ATHENAEUS, *Deipnos.* X 437b. *FGrHist* 566 a.b.

61. Schol. Aristophanes, *Birds* 436.

62. Das Kunstwerk im Zeitalter seiner technischen Reproduzierbarkeit (1936; Suhrkamp[7], 1974) 21.

63. Cf. e.g. the marble perirrhanterion with polychrome painted decoration, from a house at Olynthos (*Olynthus* XII, 1946, 246 ff. pls. 218-220). An excellent relief decoration can be seen on two marble so-called phiales from Pella (found in building fig. 8, no. 3; MAKARONAS, *AD* 16, 1960, 82 pl. 81) and from Priene (TH. WIEGAND-H. SCHRADER, *Priene* [1904] 376 f. figs 475 f.). Cf. ST. DROUGOU (*Egnatia* 1, 1989, 67 ff.), who publishes a marble table from Vergina (op. cit. pls 387-389) and a stone one from Pella (op. cit. pl. 390), and discusses such Hellenistic pieces. A marble table from 'la maison aux mosaïques': *Eretria* VIII (note 4) 44 fig. 43 (P. DUCREY).

64. ANDRONIKOS fig. 42, 156 f. ST. DROUGOU in *Ametos, for M. Andronikos* (1987) 303 ff. fig. 1 pls 63-69.

65. G. RICHTER, *Furniture* (1966) 118 fig. 589.

66. D. GERZIGER, *AntK* 18, 1975, 51 ff.

67. L. BURN, in *Greek Vases in the J. P. Getty Museum*, 5, 1991, 107 ff.

68. *CVA* Würzburg 2 pls. 42-44 fig. 43 (F. HÖLSCHER).
69. Cup Brit. Mus. *ARV²* 1269, 3. H. WALTER, *Griechische Götter* (1971) fig. 136. K. SCHEFOLD, *Die Göttersage in der klassischen und hellenistischen Kunst* (1981) figs 303-305.
70. Cf. D. RÖSSLER, Ǥab es Modetendenzen in der griech. Tracht am Ende des 5. und im 4. Jh. v.u.z.? in *Hellenische Poleis* (note 1) III, 1539 ff.
71. D. TSOUKLIDOU - V. PENNA, *AD* 34, 1979, B1 (1987) 28 ff. The mosaic is about contemporary with that at Sicyon (fig. 49), or slightly earlier. On the public baths: R. GINOUVÈS, *Balaneutikè* (1962) 184 ff. 216 ff. and passim.
72. *ARV²* 1250, 32. A. LEZZI-HAFTER, *Der Eretria-Maler* (1988) no. 253.
73. W. K. PRITCHETT, "The Attic Stelai" I (*Hesperia* 22, 1953, 225 ff.) II (ibidem 25, 1956, 178ff.). D. A. AMYX, "The Attic Stelai" III (ibidem 27, 1958, 163 ff. W. K. PRITCHETT, ibidem 30, 1961, 23 ff. D. M. LEWIS in *Ancient Society and Institutions. Studies presented to V. Ehrenberg* (1966) 177 ff.
74. As AMYX assumes (op. cit. 208).
75. PRITCHETT, op. cit. II 210.
76. W. NESTLE, ἀπραγμοσύνη (*Philologus* 81, 1926, 129-140). V. EHRENBERG, Polypragmosyne (*JHS* 67, 1947, 46-67). K. DIENELT, ἀπραγμοσύνη (*WSt* 66, 1953, 94-104). Cf. mainly EHRENBERG op. cit. and L.B. CARTER, *The Quiet Athenian* (1986) 167 ff.
77. Fig. 64: E. WALTER-KARYDI in *Kanon. Festschrift E. Berger* 15. Beih. *AntK* (1988) 331 ff. V. V. GRAEVE, ibidem 339 ff. On the subject: ibidem 332-333.
78. Cf. R. PFEIFFER, *Geschichte der klassischen Philologie* (1970) 50 ff.
79. Cf. CARTER op. cit. (note 76).
80. Cf. I. MÜLLER in *Hellenische Poleis* (note 1) III, 1389 ff. M. LANDFESTER in *Krisen in der Antike-Bewusstein und Bewährung* (1975) 27 ff. with bibl.
81. Cf. CARTER op. cit. 179 ff. H. FLASHAR in *Krisen in der Antike* (note 80) 62 ff.
82. Cf. S. HUMPHREYS, *The Family, Women and Death* (1983) 1 ff and passim. D. COHEN, *Law, Sexuality and Society. The Enforcement of Morals in Classical Athens* (1991) 70 ff.
83. In this sense the remark by F. PREISSHOFEN, 'dass die Polis durch den Andron im Oikos selbst präsent ist' (HOEPFNER-SCHWANDER 270) is, I think, right concerning the early houses with peristyle.

84. Cf. the translations: H. HITZIG in *Festgabe H. Blümner* (1914) 3.
F. PFISTER, *Die Reisebilder des Herakleides (SBWien* 227, 2, 1951) 73. M.
M. AUSTIN, *The Hellenistic World. A Selection of Ancient Sources* (1981)
151. The last phrase has been translated in various ways, e.g.
'Zeitvertreib in Menge, immerzu gibt es etwas zu schauen' (HITZIG), 'viel
Zeitvertreib und fortwährend Schaustellungen' (PFISTER), 'many
opportunities for leisure and spectacles without interruption' (AUSTIN).
However, such translations do not take into consideration the new
meaning of σχολή from the late fifth century BC onwards. Moreover, the
fact that the word is used here in the plural – while *schole* even in its
new sense, was as a rule used in the singular – and follows the mention
of philosophers, indicates that it has here the meaning that had already
appeared in Aristotle, e.g. *Politics* 1313b3, ᾽μήτε σχολὰς μήτε ἄλλους συλ-
λόγους ἐπιτρέπειν γίνεσθαι σχολαστικούς᾽, σχολαὶ meaning 'study or
discussion groups or associations'. Cf. also PLATO, *Laws* 820c and
LIDDELL-SCOTT s.v. σχολή II. The word θέα must correspondingly have
an intellectual meaning too, which is certainly a possibility from Plato
onwards, cf. e.g. ARISTOTLE, *Politeia* 209b, 20. This new meaning of
schole leads to the narrower sense the word may have from the first
century BC onwards, and from which the words scuola, école, Schule,
school..., in modern European languages derive.

85. J. BOUSQUET, *BCH* 116, 1992, 585 ff. figs 1-5 (base epigram).

Provenance of the figures

AD: 18, 19, 61. *AM*: 27, 33. *Ametos*, for M. Adronikos: 21-22. M. ANDRONIKOS, Vergina: 31. AnK: 16, 59-60. BULARD: 43. CHR. BÖRKER (*Xenia* 4): 3. J. CAMP, *Die Agora von Athen*: 1, 23. *CVA*, Berlin: 40. *CVA* Würzburg: 58. *Délos*: 7, 30, 32. École suisse d'archéologie en Grèce: 44-47, 53. *Eretria*: 6, 14, 15. Ephorate of Athens Antiquities: 62. *FdD*: 26. DAI Athens: 24-25, 48-49, 54-55. FURTWÄNGLER-REICHHOLD: 56, 63, *Hesperia*: 5, 20. W. HOEPFNER, *Das Pompeion*: 4. W. HOEPFNER - E.L. SCHWANDNER, *Haus und Stadt im klassischen Griechenland*: 2, 12, 17. Kanon (Festschrift E. Berger): 64. MAKARONAS-YOURI: 8, 9, 10, 11. J. Paul Getty Museum: 57. A. Ohnesorg: 13. Altertümer von Pergamon V1: 35. M. ROSTOVTZEFF, *Ancient Decorative Painting in South Russia* (1914, in Russia): 41-4. D. SALZMANN, *Untersuchungen zu den Kieselmosaiken*: 50. Samothrace: 36-38. M. Skiadaressis: 34, 39, 51-52, cover illustration. J. TRAVLOS, *Bildlexikon zur Topographie des antiken Athen*: 28-29.

THE BOOK *THE GREEK HOUSE:*
THE RISE OF NOBLE HOUSES
IN LATE CLASSICAL TIMES
BY ELENA WALTER-KARYDI
No 171 OF THE LIBRARY
OF THE ACHAEOLOGICAL SOCIETY AT ATHENS
WAS PRINTED IN OCTOBER 1998
AT THE PRESS
«GRAPHIKES TECHNES
E. BOULOUKOS - A. LOGOTHETIS»
26 MILONOS ST. TEL.: 93 45 204